ECKHART TOLLE'S HALL OF MIRRORS

"As someone who grew up close to the soil as a farm kid, the lessons of life, death, and relationship, were deeply instilled in me. They are lessons I take with me as a mother, wife, daughter and citizen of the world. I deeply appreciate Steve's gentle, yet resolute pushback on Tolle's message of transcendence. He champions the experience of living fully as a human and embracing the grit and grace that comes along with that journey."

—CONSTANCE CARLSON,
works in sustainable agriculture and environmental leadership, Minnesota

"Heymans compares Tolle's world view to the ideas of some classical and modern philosophers, including the themes the film director Wim Wenders explores in *Wings of Desire*. Heymans' fascinating analysis of the film shows why we humans should want to live in our temporal, physical reality rather than trying to live as supernatural beings, attempting to transcend time and our individual circumstances, as Tolle advocates."

—MARK ANEMA,
farmer, vice president,
Sustainable Farming Association of Minnesota

"Heymans puts Eckhart Tolle in his place. In a wise and adroit reading of Tolle, this book points to the deep resonances of Tolle's project with that of Plato and the long-standing problem of the search for universal transcendent forms and ideas. Heymans, following in the footsteps of Aristotle, Nussbaum, and McIntyre, brings us back down to earth, showing us the way to be fully human is to embrace the body, particularity, the place we live, and the people to whom we belong. If you have felt wary of Tolle's flight to the beyond, Heymans will help you know why."

—KATHLEEN A. CAHALAN,
professor emerita, Saint John's University, Collegeville, Minnesota

"Heymans brings his readers into a dialogue, not only with Eckhart Tolle, but with many other philosophers concerned with issues of personal identity, agency, and self-awareness. In addition to drawing upon insights from Edith Stein, George Herbert Meade, Thomas Aquinas, Martha Nussbaum, Alasdair MacIntyre, and David Abrams, Heymans critiques Tolle's "essence of all religions" through the lens of the ancient contrast between Plato and Aristotle. While Tolle aligns with the Platonic pursuit of timeless abstraction and detachment from the transient material world, Heymans argues for an Aristotelian engagement with the particulars of narrative-based physical experience, the creative and emotionally charged exploration that he sees as the truly human project."

—JIM HOFFMAN,
professor emeritus of liberal studies,
California State University Fullerton

"Steven Heymans gives serious consideration to Tolle's highly popular understanding of the nature and purpose of human existence--and shows that this understanding obscures the realities of human experience and distorts the actual conditions of human flourishing. Drawing on close readings of Tolle, his forebear Plato, and key philosophers who challenge their assumptions, Heymans rejects Tolle's emphasis on detachment and transcendence. Instead, he crafts a persuasive invitation to embrace the embodied and storied, vulnerable and relational quality of the lives we actually live with one another, in all our particularity. This book brings rich philosophical analysis to matters of constant concern, including how to understand and address anxiety and affliction. Rarely do popular spiritualities undergo such thorough and much needed analysis."

—MARK R. SCHWEHN AND DOROTHY C. BASS,
editors of *Leading Lives that Matter: What We Should Do and Who We Should Be*

Eckhart Tolle's Hall of Mirrors

A Guide to Finding Your Way Out

STEVEN HEYMANS

WIPF & STOCK · Eugene, Oregon

ECKHART TOLLE'S HALL OF MIRRORS
A Guide to Finding Your Way Out

Copyright © 2024 Steven Heymans. All rights reserved. Except for brief quotations in critical publications or reviews, no part of this book may be reproduced in any manner without prior written permission from the publisher. Write: Permissions, Wipf and Stock Publishers, 199 W. 8th Ave., Suite 3, Eugene, OR 97401.

Wipf & Stock
An Imprint of Wipf and Stock Publishers
199 W. 8th Ave., Suite 3
Eugene, OR 97401

www.wipfandstock.com

PAPERBACK ISBN: 979-8-3852-1877-6
HARDCOVER ISBN: 979-8-3852-1878-3
EBOOK ISBN: 979-8-3852-1879-0

10/23/24

For Susan Sink (1964-2024)

Contents

Preface | ix

1. Oneself as Another: Tolle's "Self-Knowledge" as Self Deception | 1
2. A Critique of Tolle's Notion of the Body | 23
3. Tolle's Disregard for the Particular | 46
4. That's Just a Story: Tolle, Plato, and Aristotle and the Use of Narrative | 74
5. Angelic Life, Foundations, and Transcendence | 96

Bibliography | 121

Preface

IT MAY BE A TRUISM to say that themes and topics of self-help books serve as indicators of a culture's self-understanding in that they both reflect and reinforce basic beliefs and identities as much by the assumptions they hold as the official advice they give. Benjamin Franklin's autobiography, for example, in saying "a penny earned saved is a penny earned" is saying something about money, to be sure, but it is also saying something about what it means to be human, and the role economics plays in it.

It has been well over two decades now since the first publishing of Eckhart Tolle's book *The Power of Now*, which was first published in 1997, and has continued to expand its presence through his subsequent books, speaking tours, and YouTube videos. Such staying power is remarkable in an industry subject to fashion not unlike clothing and food diets.

The extraordinary success of Tolle can be in great part attributed to his endorsement by Oprah Winfrey. But it cannot be denied that Tolle has struck a chord in modern audiences, has connected in a way that is due to more than mere effective marketing.

Given his success and popularity, one would think that there would be critiques of his work, which is philosophical in nature, Socratic in its style, and substantive in the sense that he is saying something that is sustained and understandable. He may jump around a bit, hinting at something here, and returning to it later. And at times there is that which does not square off with other parts of his thought. But overall he has worked out a system

Preface

(despite saying his is not a "system" but rather the straight forward "truth") and he says it well.

Critiques of his work are few and far between by scholars, perhaps because he operates on a popular level. What critiques do exist, many are less than serious, often assuming a dismissive and snarky tone all the while failing to engage him in the substance of his writing. My claim is that Tolle deserves to be taken seriously, if for no reason other than his undisputed popularity and the extent to which the content of his writing has made its way into the culture at large.

On one level, Tolle mystifies his reader with references to the Buddha, Hinduism, the Tao, and Jesus Christ. Such "cosmologies," for lack of a better word, tend to distract from the more critical aspects of Tolle's work, that being the Greek Stoics in general (in terms of their emphasis on detachment) and that of the fifth- and fourth-century BCE philosopher of Athens, Plato, in terms of his philosophy of transcending. I realize that Plato is not regarded as a Stoic in the conventional sense, but there are many Stoic qualities in Plato, and such qualities find great affinity with Tolle. The extent to which Tolle directly studied Plato, little is said. He does not include Plato among those he lists as influences. I would be surprised if he did not study Plato, but I would also not be surprised if he did not officially study Plato. I say this because Plato in many ways is the air we breathe—air that brings with it several themes that Tolle focuses on: the forms that exist beyond or behind appearances, the privileging of universal elements over that which is particular, the belief in an incorruptible soul over and against human corporeality, the notion that story-making and the emotions are at odds with rationality. Much of this comes from Plato, and the school of philosophy of which he was part at that time in Greek society. Tolle does speak openly of, and comments upon, the influence of the Greek and Roman Stoics upon his work—Marcus Aurelius, Heraclitus, Epictetus, Parmenides, and Plutarch among them. Tolle presents himself as a kind of synthesis of Buddhist, Taoist, and Hindu philosophy, which he is in his metaphysics. But it is his psychology and sociology that have had more impact upon

Preface

his readers, and that impact, so I am arguing, comes out of his appropriation of Plato. Plato, it can be said, is the philosopher of human invulnerability. He puts forth a philosophy of psychology that empowers his students to disidentify with the many earthly forms that are unstable, subject to change, and compels us to identify with that which is permanent and stable. Institutions, memory, bodies, emotions, desire are problematic for Tolle in the very same way they were for Plato.

That Plato and Aristotle are often mentioned in the same breadth gives the impression that they are like-minded in their philosophies, resulting in our failure to appreciate the extent to which Aristotle was a critic of Plato. And it is the case, so I am arguing, that the criticism Aristotle makes of Plato applies equally to the neo-Platonist Tolle. In this somewhat roundabout way, Tolle provide us with a fresh way to understand and appreciate Aristotle. For example, in contrast to Tolle's "rising above" and theme of detachment as a way of living a less troubled life, Aristotle argues that human attachment to persons and objects of this world is simply the human way; a life that is otherwise is not available to us. As long as humans are embodied and mortal creatures, this will be the case.

It should be added that a more frequent contrast dealt with in this book is the difference between Tolle's (and Plato's) method of universalizing, in contrast to Aristotle's emphasis upon particulars. In this conversation, I employ other thinkers, all of whom I regard as Aristotelian in temperament (such as Edith Stein, George Herbert Mead, and David Abram), but who may not be officially "neo-Aristotelian" (unlike Martha Nussbaum and Alasdair MacIntyre). But, at the end of the day, the critique of Tolle is hopefully a sustained one, and one that is in one way or another representative of Aristotle. And by providing such a contrast, Tolle's self-help project provides a relief that highlights the content and beauty of Aristotle's project of how one should live. In this way this book is a "guide" for finding one's way out of Tolle's "hall of mirrors" and into the terrestrial life of mortals.

Preface

It is with very mixed feelings that I write this preface, after having of course written the individual chapters prior to writing the preface. Such mixed emotions are due to the fact that I spent many nights and days of the last eight months overseeing and participating in my wife's hospice care at our home in central Minnesota. Themes of human vulnerability, dependence, and bodily corruptibility have been on full display as I have written the chapters of this book. At the same time, this has been a time of richness and inspiration, seeing how Susan accepts with grace and equanimity the corruptibility that is brought about by ovarian cancer. In addition to this, she has been a first line of criticism in terms of the development and editing of this book. Her insights and suggestions have benefited me invaluably, as well as her encouragement. In addition to Susan, I would like to thank theologians Kevin Mongrain and John Merkle for their generosity of time and talent in the reading and revision of this book. John's careful reading and feedback, and Kevin's ability to organize themes, made this a much more readable and coherent book.

And lastly, I wish to thank the two students of Aristotle—Martha Nussbaum and Alasdair MacIntyre—whose appropriation of Aristotle have been foundational for me personally and have provided a model of practical reasoning that have made the writing of this book possible.

1

Oneself as Another

Tolle's "Self-Knowledge" as Self Deception

AN ECONOMICAL WAY OF engaging Tolle's understanding of self is to begin with a story he tells about the "false self," a retelling of the Greek mythological account of Narcissus, in which he says:

> One day Narcissus looked into a pool of water and he was fascinated by his own reflection; the story says that he fell in love with himself, with his own reflection. The story says that he fell in love with himself but my interpretation is really that he became obsessed, not with himself, but with the image of himself. . . . What it points to is the arising of the human ego, which is a kind of phantom self you carry around that you mistake for who you actually are.[1]

"How you are seen by others," Tolle writes elsewhere, "becomes the mirror that tells you what you are like and who you are. The ego's sense of self-worth is in most cases bound up with the worth you have in the eyes of others. You need others to give you a sense of self."[2] In Tolle's account, what Narcissus saw in the mirror was not himself, but an image of himself constructed by others—an image

---

1. Tolle, "Prison of Narcissism."
2. Tolle, *New Earth*, 45.

Eckhart Tolle's Hall of Mirrors

that is, by Tolle's definition, a "false self," because it came from others and not from one's direct experience. As Tolle puts it, this is

> an externally derived sense of self. That is to say, you get your sense of who you are from things that ultimately have nothing to do with who you are, your social role, possessions, external appearance, success and failures, belief systems and so on. This false, mind-made self feels vulnerable, insecure and is always seeking new things to identify with to give it a feeling that it exists.[3]

From Tolle's perspective, this "mind-made" constructed self is brought about through compulsive thinking—the thinking chatter that characterizes much of our waking hours. Such thinking chatter contributes to a "fragmentation of mind"[4] that can be corrected through one's becoming whole again. There are many words for this process of becoming whole again—enlightenment, awakening, consciousness, wholeness, presence, oneness, awareness, mindfulness—all of which is made possible by one's connecting with, and experience of "Being," a notion that is eternal, or outside of our human experience of time.

As Tolle puts it, humans are naturally aware of a primordial oneness of creation, but this awareness and experience of Being and the primordial oneness is lost as we go about our lives creating and bolstering our own identity, which we do by identifying with things in the world around us. Also, as we identify with objects outside ourselves, there comes a reactivity, resistance, and separateness between our mind/bodies and the world around us. To make matters worse, this mind/body reactivity gets covered up by thinking, and we become a thinking mind/body that becomes unaware of this reactivity. But beneath the mind/body is Being, which lies at the center of reality, and is beyond the matter of our bodies and the thought that covers up that matter. Being is spiritual, and not physical, and as a spirit it is not contained within the body but is everywhere. Being is universal, and in discovering that Being within oneself, one discovers one's "true self."

3. Tolle, *Power of Now*, 150–51.
4. Tolle, *Power of Now*, 15.

Oneself as Another

Just as thinking can cover one's awareness of Being, so time can cover up one's awareness of Being. As Tolle puts it, "The mind, to ensure that it remains in control, seeks continuously to cover up the present moment with past and future, and so, as the vitality and infinite creative potential of Being, which is inseparable from the Now, becomes covered up by time, your true nature becomes obscured by the mind."[5]

Tolle presents time, or temporality, as at odds with Being. His criticism of temporality—or, said differently, his criticism of human agents who think historically in terms of their personal identity—is that it ends up shaping our identities, informing us, and in doing this limits our freedom. The way our time thinking shapes our identity is through "forms" that it imposes upon us. And forms are preexisting boxes that are given to us, that we inherit, so to speak, into which we put our ideas about ourselves, the world, and others. Living in time means living in a world that gives us boxes into which we fit our thoughts, actions, and things. And the ego, the false self, really believes that these forms into which we put our ideas about ourselves are real. This attachment to forms is at the heart of the problem, as Tolle puts it, for "ego is no more than this: identification with form, which primarily means through thought forms. If evil has any reality—and it has a relative, not an absolute, reality—this also is its definition: complete identification with form—physical forms, thought forms, emotional forms."[6]

In our becoming aware of Being, we find ourselves no longer contained within time and, in so doing, no longer operating from an egoic, historically-informed understanding of self. Once we become aware of Being, we can transcend the thinking mind/body and see ourselves and the world around us as they are, not as we have been conditioned to see them by the forms that have been imposed upon us.

Narcissus fell in love not with himself, but with an image of himself. Tolle's argument here is that those who look to others to tell them who they are do so out of a deep insecurity, attempting

5. Tolle, *Power of Now*, 34.
6. Tolle, *New Earth*, 22.

to secure a sense of themselves. But in doing this, they end up with a false self. This "externally derived sense of self" comes from an unconscious acceptance of one's social role and assigned institutional forms. To accept the social forms that are given is to create a "false, mind-made self"[7] that is characterized by delusion, conflict, pain, and separateness. As for one's "true self," this is found in Being, that which transcends forms, identity, time, and the historical conditioning that comes with it.

EDITH STEIN ON SELF KNOWLEDGE

Empathy, like narcissism, tends to be interpreted and discussed in psychological categories, and is often presented in opposition to, and a corrective of, narcissism. It is perhaps not coincidental that Edith Stein's philosophy of empathy, that is at the center of her understanding of self-knowledge, contrasts sharply with Tolle's notion of self-knowledge.

Edith Stein's legacy is one of richness. She was born in what is now Poland but spent most of her adult life in Germany at the turn of the twentieth century. She was a Jewish convert to Catholicism, a student of German philosophy, particularly that of phenomenology, in which she received a doctorate at a time when few women were admitted into graduate programs (and no women were allowed to teach in German universities), and afterward studied and wrote about Catholic theology and spirituality. She eventually became a Carmelite nun, and she, along with her biological sister, were murdered in a German death camp in 1941. In 2001 she was made a saint in the Roman Catholic Church.

Stein's philosophical work centered around the concept of empathy, the topic of her graduate thesis, in which she examined the essential character of what makes for one's empathic awareness of others, an awareness that, when practiced, enhances one's own self-knowledge.

---

7. Tolle, *Power of Now*, 150–51.

Critical to her overall project is putting forth an account of the mind/body relationship in which she asserts that the *I* that I experience as consciousness inhabits a particular body. By thinking of one's self as an embodied self, she encourages us to see human consciousness not so much as the "psychic" activity of one's mind, but as a "psycho-physical" activity in our bodies.[8] As she puts it, "For greater clarity here, we must now take a step that we have been reluctant to take until the course of the investigation demanded it. This is the step from psychic to psycho-physical. Our proposed division between soul and body was an artificial one, for the soul is always necessarily a soul in a body. What is the body? How is it given to us?"[9] Her answer is that, on the one hand, one can give a very general description of consciousness—that it involves "outer perception," for example. But a better description, says Stein, is that consciousness is an act of this *particular* me—as *my* seeing—and the object that I am experiencing. As she puts it, "the relationship between seeing and touching is different here than anywhere else. Everything else I see says to me, 'Touch me.' I am really what I seem to be, am tangible, and not a phantom. And what I touch calls to me, 'Open your eyes and you will see me.'"[10] Stein's notion of consciousness is not a generic "outer consciousness," a third-person detached experience; rather it is a first-person experiencing self from this body with that object.

A big part of Stein's project was exploring in detail where and how one inhabits a body. For example, she asks herself if she is more in her torso than in her extremities, if this part of her body can be considered more here than there. The place in her body that she can say most approximates where she is, she calls the "zero point of orientation."[11] "Not only do I possess an inner space," she writes, but

> all the objects in the outer world have a certain distance from me. They are always "there" while I am always here.

---

8. Stein, *On the Problem of Empathy*, 40.
9. Stein, *On the Problem of Empathy*, 40–41.
10. Stein, *On the Problem of Empathy*, 41.
11. Stein, *On the Problem of Empathy*, 43.

They are grouped around me, around my "here." As my living body moves around, the objects in my sphere move, increasing and decreasing in size, and reveal themselves to me from other perspectives: Every step I take discloses a new bit of the world to me or I see the old one from a new side. In so doing I always take my living body along. Not only am I always here, but also it is; the various "distances" of its parts from me are only variations with this "here."[12]

However, the distance of one's body parts in relation to one's zero point that one experiences pales in comparison to the living body of other "foreign physical bodies,"[13] which is to say that the *I*, here, in my body must acknowledge the distance of you, there, as an embodied self that is "other" or "foreign" to me. For Stein there is a dramatic distinction between my body and objects in the world around me, but that dramatic distinction is even more pronounced when we talk about other persons—"foreign physical bodies"—as she puts it: "The living body as a whole is at a zero point of orientation with all physical bodies outside of it. 'Body space' and 'outer space' are completely different from each other. Merely perceiving outwardly, I would not arrive at a living body, nor merely 'perceiving bodily' at the outer world."[14]

So, what is it that allows us to see other bodies as not just part of the mix of objects in the world outside of myself? What is it, Stein asks, that allows me to experience others as bodies possessing their own subjectivity, as others, like us but separate living bodies? "The living body," she writes, "cannot be separated from the givenness of the spatial outer world. The other's physical body as a mere physical body is spatial like other things and is given at a

---

12. Stein, *On the Problem of Empathy*, 47.

13. Stein, *On the Problem of Empathy*, 43. Waltraut Stein completed her translation of *On the Problem of Empathy* in 1964 at a time when Emmanuel Levinas's work was beginning to make its way into philosophical discourse. One cannot help but think that, had she translated the book a decade or two later, she would have translated "foreign physical bodies" employing the term "otherness" in some form in this context.

14. Stein, *On the Problem of Empathy*, 43.

certain location, at a certain distance, from me as the center of spatial orientation, and in certain spatial relationships to the rest of the spatial world. When I now interpret it as a sensing living body and empathetically project myself into it, I obtain a new image."[15]

In other words, I perceive empathically when I can experience my spatial reality of me at its center—that of my body *here*—but at the same time have knowledge of another body's spatial reality and of it having a center for whom I am its *there*. At this point I think of the other, not as an object in proximity to my subject, but another subject to me, just as I am a subject to it:

"From the viewpoint of zero point orientation gained in empathy, I must no longer consider my own zero point as *the* zero point, but as *a* spatial point among many. By this means, and only by this means, I learn to see my living body as a physical body like others."[16]

"I cannot look at myself freely as at another physical body,"[17] she writes. That is, I cannot be an object of my own subjectivity, but rather I must learn to see myself as one "spatial point among many." In this way I can come to realize that I am not a part that fits into a whole, but am a whole that is incomplete, lacking in fullness; I am a whole among other wholes in the form of other physical bodies. Thus, the other becomes a mirror for me, a mirror on which I depend to assist me in seeing myself more fully. As Stein puts it, "This reiterative empathy is at the same time the condition making possible that mirror-image-like givenness of myself in memory and fantasy on which we have touched several times."[18]

Stein goes on to say that it is possible that my interpretations of myself can be wrong, and that empathically attending to the world around us can serve as a "corrective" of such misperceptions. Indeed, "it is possible for another to judge me more accurately than I judge myself."[19]

---

15. Stein, *On the Problem of Empathy*, 60.
16. Stein, *On the Problem of Empathy*, 63.
17. Stein, *On the Problem of Empathy*, 63.
18. Stein, *On the Problem of Empathy*, 63.
19. Stein, *On the Problem of Empathy*, 89.

Eckhart Tolle's Hall of Mirrors

For Stein, other bodies within my space function as a mirror to me, a mirror image that I must interpret through use of my memory and imagination. It is by and through memory and imagination that I have, over time, come to construct an idea of myself that is accountable to feedback, as it were, that I have been given in bits and pieces. Seeing ourselves in the mirror of others, though still a first-person experience, does not deprive us of the third-person experience of us by others. It is still me experiencing the "other." But knowing this allows me to pay attention to the other, especially what they tell me by how they look and communicate with me. It is this going back and forth, out to the other and then back to oneself, in which we weigh, process, assimilate, and therefore grow in self-knowledge and consciousness. It is through this interaction between the first-person me and third-person other that the habit and practice of empathy is brought about in myself.

Tolle argues that we should rid ourselves of the voices of the third-person others who play a role, as Stein argues, in becoming who we are. From the Narcissus myth we learned that Tolle approves of our having an "I" but he does not approve of an "I" that is informed by the voices of others telling me who my "I" is. Tolle extends this argument in a slightly different way when he talks about the "self" in which, he asks, if I already am an "I," why do I need a "self," such as when I speak of "I" and "myself?" To talk this way suggests having two selves. And to have two selves—the "I" and the "myself"—is to create a split, a "duality," within oneself. Tolle writes,

> This mind-created duality is the root cause of all unnecessary complexity, of all problems and conflicts in your life. In the state of enlightenment, you are yourself—"you" and "yourself" merge into one. You do not judge yourself, you do not feel sorry for yourself, you are not proud of yourself, you do not love yourself, you do not hate yourself, and so on. The split caused by self-reflective consciousness is healed, its curse removed. There is no "self" that you need to protect, defend, or feed anymore. When you are enlightened, there is one relationship that you no longer have: the relationship with yourself. Once

you have given that up, all your other relationships will be love relationships.[20]

Tolle describes this duality as a kind of "curse" and "madness," and the form this curse takes is of an inner dialogue between one's "I" and "myself":

> When someone goes to the doctor and says, "I hear a voice in my head," he or she will most likely be sent to a psychiatrist. The fact is that, in a very similar way, virtually everyone hears a voice, or several voices, in their head all the time: the involuntary thought processes that you don't realize you have the power to stop.... You have probably come across "mad" people in the street incessantly talking or muttering to themselves. Well that's not much different from what you and all other "normal" people do, except that you don't do it out loud. The voice comments, speculates, judges, compares, likes, dislikes, and so on.[21]

From Stein's perspective, this "voice in our head" comes to us as an "other" through imagination and memory and with whom we dialogue. Such an inner dialogue is not the madness that Tolle calls it; rather, it is what Stein considers the normal human way in which we acquire an empathic self. What Stein argued for philosophically, we can examine more specifically through the work of social psychologist George Herbert Mead, whose work at the turn of the nineteenth century complements and extends that of Stein's.[22]

Mead puts forth the argument that language and communication is a critical part of being a human—that humans are linguistic creatures to the core—and that we are in communication with others, even when they are not present. Dialogue and monologue with others is ongoing, in part because, over time, we internalize these conversations with others—what they say becomes part of an inner, ongoing, and collective conversation. Such a conversation

20. Tolle, *Power of Now*, 174–75.

21. Tolle, *Power of Now*, 17.

22. Much of what I am using from Mead comes from his *Mind, Self, and Society*.

begins in our childhood, a time when we learn what it is to be a self through the imitation of others. What children imitate in play are not personalities so much as character roles, about which Mead writes,

> In the play period the child utilizes his own responses to these stimuli which he makes use of in building a self. The response which he has a tendency to make to these stimuli organizes them. He plays that he is, for example, offering himself something, and he buys it; he gives a letter to himself and takes it away; he addresses himself as a parent, as a teacher; arrests himself as a policeman. He has a set of stimuli which call out to himself the sort of responses they call out in others. He takes the group of responses and organizes them into a certain whole. Such is the simplest form of being another to one's self. It involves a temporal situation. The child says something in one character, and responds in another character, and then his responding in another character is a stimulus to himself in the first character, and so the conversation goes on. A certain organized structure arises in him and in his other which replies to it, and these carry on the conversation of gestures between themselves.[23]

Mead makes the case that there is another level of subjectivity to be learned by the child through games: "If we contrast play with the situation in an organized game, we note the essential difference that the child who plays in a game must be ready to take the attitude of everyone else involved in that game, and that these different roles or positions must have a definite relationship to each other."[24] In games or sports, such as baseball, a child learns that not only are there other players, but each player has a position on the field, each with its own space and responsibilities. To develop as a baseball player is to, in part, develop a sensitivity to these other positions on the field in a way that we come to view our role as a player in the context of all the other players' positions on the field as a whole.

23. Mead, *Mind, Self, and Society*, 150–51.
24. Mead, *Mind, Self, and Society*, 151.

Oneself as Another

To be a subject is to be the me that is perceiving. To be an object is to be the other that I, the subject, perceive. Whereas Edith Stein argues that in recognizing the otherness of an embodied other self, we can come to see them as subjects, as we are a subject; Mead argues this a bit differently by saying that another "enters his own experience as a self or individual, not directly or immediately, not by becoming a subject to himself, but only insofar as he first becomes an object to himself just as other individuals are objects to him or in his experience; and he becomes an object to himself only by taking the attitudes of other individuals toward himself within a social environment or context of experience and behavior in which both he and they are involved."[25] In this way we learn to see ourselves as we see others—as objects that are at some distance from me. I am suggesting that Stein and Mead are saying the same thing but in different ways: that we come to have a self and see ourselves more truthfully through the process of engaging another who then becomes incorporated into oneself. In this way we are, as Paul Ricoeur puts it, *Oneself as Another*.[26]

This other within oneself is a composite of many voices in one's personal history, but takes the form of a singular voice, which Mead calls the "generalized other." One's conversation with one's generalized other is a conversation with oneself, in effect, in which our other functions as a kind of sounding board so that we might hear our own voice. Upon hearing our own voice, in terms of, say, some future conversation, Mead says, we might find ourselves saying "that sounded harsh; let's try a different approach," and so we adjust accordingly.

It is with our generalized other that we evaluate past events and strategize future engagements. And once one's generalized other and oneself have formulated a good rationale for this or that, we then bring our strategy, as it were, to an imagined audience. Such an audience is generally those who may be involved with the topic at hand, for example, coworkers debating a business place issue, or family members in sibling disputes. This is an important

---

25. Mead, *Mind, Self, and Society*, 138.
26. Ricoeur, *Oneself as Another*.

element in one's project of becoming a responsible human as the audience represents a third party, a kind of jury to whom we more or less successfully make a reasoned argument. Such a dynamic is an important step in one's psychological process because it recreates a world outside ourself to which we strive to be accountable.

Some have accused Mead of being a social determinist, a school of psychology that says there is nothing in the self that might transcend one's environment and history. But this is not the case in that Mead makes a distinction between the "I" and the "myself." Continuing with the baseball game metaphor, we know that at some point, a batter is going to hit the ball and I am going have to make a play. The "myself" is that me that has internalized the positions and responsibilities of my teammates as a whole over time. Another way of saying this is that this "myself" is the social and historical me, embedded in the field of play with a sense of the overall game. The "I" is the me that spontaneously lunges for the ball, catches and throws the ball to second base in hopes of making a double play, rather than throwing out the runner at first base. The "I" is the me that pre-reflectively responds and cannot be anticipated. Once the "I" has directed the act, the act becomes part of the "myself," part of the repertoire of my possible responses in baseball, or in the classroom, or in the family dining room.

For Mead, there is an interplay between the "myself" that has acquired habits, responses, tools for engagement in the world, and the "I" that directs this skilled and socialized "myself." Even though there is much that is consistent with oneself—that we act in character most of the time, and not out of character—there are moments when we, directed by the "I," act in ways that surprise even ourselves.

In Mead's scheme of things, the "I" is not determined by conditioning, but at the same time it is not a transcendent ego, totally outside of one's experience and beyond the generalized others. The "talk in our head" that Tolle diagnoses as "madness," and for which he claims to have a cure, is for Mead a natural human dynamic of an ongoing dialogue between an "I" and the various groups of generalized others from my history. This inner dialogue of "oneself as another," is the result of human socialization, and is something that contributes to our becoming a responsible human being.

As stated earlier, Tolle's position contrasts with that of Stein and Mead's in which he would say they are dualistic—that they take what should be one and singular—the "I"—and make it two or multiple—the "I" and "Myself." There is truth to this, Mead would say, that the notion of self he describes phenomenologically assumes multiple elements. As Mead writes,

> Normally, within the sort of community as a whole to which we belong, there is a unified self, but that may be broken up. To a person who is somewhat unstable nervously and in whom there is a line of cleavage, certain activities become impossible, and that set of activities may separate and evolve another self. Two separate "me's" and "I's," two different selves, results, and that is the condition under which there is a tendency to break up the personality. There is an account of a professor of education who disappeared and was lost to the community, and later turned up at a logging camp in the West. He freed himself from his occupation and turned up in the woods where he felt, if you like, more at home.[27]

This passage is interesting for two reasons. First, it demonstrates the fragility of the self, of personal identity, and that the "me" and "myself" can become two selves, as Tolle says. On the other hand, from our human experience we can see that our inclination is toward a single self, but with multiple others working within it that Mead describes. At the same time, the one self that we are inclined toward must be maintained through memory, community, and the many forms that Tolle disparages, indeed seeks to dispossess us of. Tolle considers this maintenance of self as ego intensifying, and therefore promotes its dispossession, arguing that only then can we discover one's true self. In response, I argue this is not human, is not the way the human mind works, and will argue this in more detail in chapter 5 of this book.

---

27. Mead, *Mind, Self, and Society*, 143.

For now, in response to Tolle, let us say that multiple elements do arise in ourselves through the socialization process we discussed, but such multiplicity is contained within a larger operating "I" that is singular. In this way we can say there is a duality that is contained within a non-duality of a singular or unified self.

TOLLE'S THIRD-PERSON TRANSCENDENT SELF

Tolle uses the same scheme of self and other as Stein and Mead, in terms of how self-knowledge is brought about. However the *other* as *other* represents a problem for Tolle because otherness should not exist in a created order in which Being is the ultimate reality, a creation where oneness is the operative category. Experience of the *other* as *other*, for Tolle, is a misrecognition, and to recognize them properly is to see that there is in fact no otherness, that everything is within the oneness of Being. For Stein and Mead, the other's otherness is real, not an illusion because, as embodied selves, the substance of their body can never be the substance of my body at the same time.

In *The Power of Now* and *A New Earth* Tolle encourages us to speak, in terms of the experience of our day-to-day lives, not in the voice of first person, but in the third person, from an omniscient point of view. The first-person "I-spoken" voice is to be avoided, for Tolle, because it comes from the various forms that sustain the ego:

> When a young child learns that a sequence of sounds produced by the parents' vocal cords is his or her name, the child begins to equate a word, which in the mind becomes a thought, with who he or she is. At that stage, some children refer to themselves in the third person. "Johnny is hungry." Soon after, they learn the magic word "I" and equate it with their name which they have already equated with who they are. Then other thoughts come and merge with the I-thought. The next step are thoughts of me and mine to designate things that are somehow part of "I." . . . And so when the child grows up, the original I-thought attracts other thoughts to itself: It becomes

identified with a gender, possessions, the sense-perceived body, nationality, race, religion, profession. Other things "I" identifies with are roles—mother, father, husband, wife, and so on—accumulated knowledge or opinions, likes and dislikes and also things that happened to me in the past, the memory of which are thoughts that further define my sense of self as "me and my story."[28]

In this way Tolle's account of human development is that of psychological movement from a third-person view of self, in which the child thinks and addresses himself from the outside, to a first-person view of self, in which the third-person movement to first-person is from one of less identification with form to more identification. This movement from less to more identification with form, from third-person to first-person thinking, represents for Tolle, an expansion of egoic/false-self. In other words, for Tolle, self-knowledge is realized as one transcends to a third-person point of view.

Put differently: "If you are content being nobody in particular," he writes, "you align yourself with the power of the universe."[29] In other words, for Tolle, the more one can separate from one's particular body, and adopt the point of view of anybody, the more conscious, aware, and enlightened one is. And of course the more one sees oneself as a particular body, which is to say as one among other bodies (as Stein would have it), the more unconscious one is, the more one operates out of a false self.

In defense of himself, Tolle might say, does not the "generalized other" of Mead, and the "other body" of Stein, represent a kind of third-party, omniscient point of view? In response we say they are not. They represent particular other human beings, sometimes composites, sometime individuals, whose view has contributed to our first-person point of view. The two positions are quite opposed in that Tolle's third party is an omniscient "nobody," a disembodied spirit.

---

28. Tolle, *New Earth*, 29.
29. Tolle, *New Earth*, 216.

Eckhart Tolle's Hall of Mirrors

Stein would add that Tolle's transcendent third person is indeed not a person at all. If it were a person, it would be embodied. It presents a problem because, as Stein's central thesis has it, our consciousness is an embodied consciousness, that our thoughts and experience come through our bodies, and that we are inseparable from our bodies. In other words, I cannot experience objects or persons out there in the world directly, unmediated, circumventing my body. If this was the case, it would no longer be me doing the experiencing; the objects and persons I experience, are experienced by me—a particular body with a particular name, gender, set of roles, and history.

In this way one cannot speak of that which is universal—like Being, for example—in an unqualified way, because it is me, a me who lives in a particular body in a particular time and place, who is doing the listening and speaking about Being. The body that is physically diminished, injured, ill, or stressed will experience Being differently from a body that is vigorous, healthy, and active, perhaps even to the extent that we can no longer describe such agents as experiencing the same thing. Such different experiences of Being calls into question Tolle's argument for the unchanging, timeless, immutable nature of Being. Moreover, what I know about Being has been taught to me by others who themselves are bodies who were born in particular places and are of particular ages, all of which they bring to our conversation about Being. In this way, when we do our speaking about Being, or that which is universal, we must acknowledge, Stein would say, that it is me or us that is doing the speaking, a me that is an embodied, human animal me, and let us acknowledge what we bring our experience to what is "universal."

The same can be said with Tolle's notion of the "eternal *now.*" Tolle's argument is that we can transcend time and access an eternal non-time through experiencing the now, the present. Stein's understanding of the embodied nature of human life brings with it the belief that you can be present all you want, but it's still *you* being present—a you in a particular body, with a particular history, with particular language, with particular aspirations, and with a particular array of experience. The you that is in the now is an interpreting you and that interpreting invariably involves particularity.

The same can be said of much that is referred to as *universal*. What is "universal" about universal, it can be said, is that my understanding of universal is one that I arrived at through thought and conversation with other embodied consciousnesses who corrected and contributed to *this* understanding of universal, a notion that is now shared between myself and others. Thus it is important to say that, because my understanding of something universal had to be appropriated through my particular body, does not mean that we are therefore relegated to a morally radical individualism, indifferent to, and failing to factor in, the existence of others. This understanding of a shared engagement with others, one that generates reflection, revision, and the possibility for cooperation, Edith Stein and her mentor, Edmund Husserl, described as "intersubjective." Stein's second criticism would be that, even if we could detach, step back, and act as a third-person, omniscient observer, such an act would have the effect of neutralizing our agency as persons. As Martin Heidegger put it in *Being and Time*, we are "bodily" and such bodiliness has a threefold quality in relation to the world—thrownness, fallenness, and projection.[30] All three terms here overlap in an attempt to promote the singular idea— that as bodily creatures we are deeply embedded, if not forced into, the materiality of this world. Such thrownness into the matter of the world defines Being, not as a timeless, nowhere-in-particular place, but as human beings in the world. Devoid of such corporeality—of such bodiliness in the world—and recast as detached observers, our human agency is neutralized. In other words, to have agency is to recognize and embrace our corporeality. Such recognition and such an embrace are characterized by our ability to speak in the first person.

---

30. Heidegger, *Being and Time*, 284.

ECKHART TOLLE AND NARCISSISM

This chapter began with Tolle's (re)telling of the Narcissus myth. The original story had it that Narcissus fell in love with his own image in a pool of water and became so transfixed by the beauty of his own image that he eventually pined away. In Tolle's version of the story, "he became so obsessed, not with himself, but with the image of himself." From this Tolle concludes, "What it points to is the arising of the human ego which is a kind of phantom self you carry around that you mistake for who you really are."[31]

In this way, Tolle's project is one of empowering us to see ourselves as who we are, and not who others tell us we are. We accomplish this by looking in a mirror—not the mirror of other people, as Edith Stein would have it, but a mirror that is, as it were, transparent—a mirror of awareness. The problem is that awareness, as an end in itself, ends up being a hall of mirrors. How is this the case?

As said earlier, in terms of Tolle's line of thinking, that which functions as an obstacle between oneself and Being, is the egoic mind, which compels us to identify with our thoughts. Awareness is the means by which we overcome the thinking-self ego, an awareness of our obsessive thinking: "The moment you start watching the thinker, a higher level of consciousness becomes activated. . . . You begin to awaken."[32]

Likewise, what is true of thinking, Tolle writes, can also be said of the emotions, which "will be reflected in the body as an emotion and of this you can become aware." Once this happens, "you no longer *are* the emotion; you are the watcher, the observing presence. If you practice this, all that is unconscious in you will be brought into the light of consciousness."[33] And so awareness is created by appointing a watcher of one's thinking, and a watcher of one's emotions activates in us a "higher level of consciousness."

---

31. Tolle, "Prison of Narcissism."
32. Tolle, *Power of Now*, 17.
33. Tolle, *Power of Now*, 37.

Oneself as Another

What Tolle says about the watcher of thinking and the emotions is that the watcher is unwatched, that the agent is unaware of the watcher. The point is that, as various philosophers have said, the subject cannot be an object to itself, which is to say that the watcher cannot watch and be the object watched at the same time.

What can be said about Tolle's watcher of thought and emotions can also be said about roles we inhabit. The problem with roles, he writes, is that they are forms, to be sure, but are all the more insidious because over time they take us over. That is to say, the newly hired professor, over time, becomes all the more professorial; the mother of a newborn becomes, over time, all the more maternal. As a corrective to this, Tolle advises, "don't try to be anybody in particular. You are most powerful, most effective, when you are completely yourself. But don't try to be yourself. That's another role. It's called 'natural, spontaneous me.' As soon as you are trying to be this or that, you are playing a role."[34] Such advice invites the criticism of how is it that trying not to "just be yourself" avoids being but another role? The answer is that it doesn't, and that the rejection "just being yourself" is the role of the non, nonconformist. And so it goes.

Likewise, Tolle writes, "When you become conscious of Being, what is really happening is that Being becomes conscious of itself. When Being becomes present of itself—that's presence. Since Being, consciousness, and life are synonymous, we could say that presence means consciousness becoming conscious of itself, or of life attaining self-consciousness."[35]

Readers who take these words seriously, so I am arguing, will find themselves in a hall of mirrors, the self, looking at the self, looking at the self. Christopher Lasch, over some forty years ago, in his book *The Culture of Narcissism*, describes this dynamic as a *regressus in infinitum*, "in which the writer," for example, "withdraws from his subject but at the same time becomes so conscious of these distancing techniques that he finds it more and more difficult

---

34. Tolle, *New Earth*, 108.
35. Tolle, *Power of Now*, 98.

to write about anything except the difficulty of writing."[36] Such a dynamic gives rise to what Lasch calls an "ironic detachment" that distances us from the world we inhabit and diminishes our power as agents of social change in both our immediate, as well as in our larger political environment. Such distancing through ironic detachment becomes "itself an illusion; at best it provides only momentary relief. Distancing soon becomes a routine in its own right. Awareness commenting on awareness creates an escalating cycle of self-consciousness that inhibits spontaneity."[37] Ironically this "escalating cycle of self-consciousness" that Tolle creates becomes at one and the same time the very "Prison of Narcissism" from which he claims to free us. When "consciousness" is undirected, that is, when it has no object outside the self, and thus nothing to move oneself toward in action, it by default turns into "self-consciousness," thereby becoming a hall of mirrors—a *regressus in infinitum*—from which there is no escape without outside intervention.

Lasch argues that "self-awareness" and "ironic self-detachment" in fact form an illusion that is characteristic of the modern, or new, narcissist. Such "ironic self-detachment" ends up being illusory for the "self-aware" in that it gives the narcissist the sense that "although he assumes that it is impossible to alter the iron limits imposed upon him by society, a detached awareness of those limits seems to make them matter less. By demystifying daily life, he conveys to himself and others the impression that he has risen above it, even as he goes through the motions and does what is expected of him."[38] And this, of course, is the appeal and the genius of Tolle's spiritual teaching: that, unlike the ordinary, unconscious selves around us, we—"the new consciousness that lives in the transcendence of thought"[39]—live in what is real.

It is worth returning at this point to Stein's argument—that the embodied selves that we are afford us no omniscient, transcendent

36. Lasch, *Culture of Narcissism*, 118.
37. Lasch, *Culture of Narcissism*, 117.
38. Lasch, *Culture of Narcissism*, 116.
39. Tolle, *New Earth*, 21.

place from which to view our self and our situation, that one's experiencing is from a particular place on the ground level, as it were. Thus, the sense that one has "risen above it," which is to say, to see oneself as experiencing the world from a privileged, transcendent place, is an illusion that is characteristic of grandiose narcissism. Seeing oneself as viewing life from a transcendent perspective is a point of view that fails to locate itself as that of a particular body with a particular zero point and, in so doing, excludes from itself the history, substances, criteria, categories, externalities on which its claims depend. As Tolle puts it:

> This book [*The Power of Now*] can be seen as a restatement for our time of that one timeless spiritual teaching, the essence of all religions. It is not derived from external sources, but from the one true source within, so it contains no theory or speculation. I speak from inner experience, and if at times I speak forcefully, it is to cut through the heavy layers of mental resistance and to reach that place within you where you already *know*, just as I know, and where the truth is recognized when it is heard. There is then a feeling of exaltation and heightened aliveness, as something within you says: "Yes, I know this is true."[40]

Such claims to be "the essence of all religions," and containing "no theory or speculation," but rather being "the one true source within," serve to mystify and neutralize the listener through the exclusion of external sources such as history, literature, philosophy from the conversation. Indeed, such claims are put forth as givens, self-evident truths for which there is no need to provide explanation.

The tone is that Tolle is merely a vessel, merely channeling what we already know within our deepest selves, or should know, if we are operating out of the non-egoic, authentic self. As for those who do not recognize such claims in their own experience and way of thinking, or may find such claims problematic, the problem does not reside in the nature of these claims, but in the nature of the listener who, no doubt, must be operating out of the "dysfunction

---

40. Tolle, *Power of Now*, 10.

of the egoic human mind,"[41] a false, egoic self that possesses a point of view that cannot be trusted, particularly by the subject herself. Not getting it, they are being told, means simply that they have more spiritual work to do.

---

41. Tolle, *New Earth*, 21.

2

A Critique of Tolle's Notion of the Body

WHAT TOLLE SAYS ABOUT the egoic mind—that it serves as a prison that prevents us from accessing Being/Consciousness—he also says about the body, which operates as a prison of our souls, so to speak. Just as the mental images, roles, memories, and stories we tell about ourselves have little to do with our true selves, for Tolle, our physical bodies have little to do with our true selves. In contrast to Tolle, I will argue in this chapter that the body presents itself as a most stubborn obstacle to Tolle's project of disidentification and transcendence because of its irreducible, concrete, and particular form. That is, it cannot be reduced to anything less and still be a body; nor can it be a body in general as all bodies are particular—as in myself, as an embodied human, and you, as an embodied person. No matter how I might try, the experience of my body here is not your experience of your body there.

Our experience of the particularity of our body as one and singular presents a challenge for Tolle, but equally challenging to Tolle's project is the temporality of the body—that the body exists in time, which is to say that bodily existence comes to an end. To exist in time is to say that the body has a beginning and an end. And between this beginning and end, we find another development:

there will be a time of dependence as infants and children, followed by a brief period of maturity, relative self-sufficiency, and independence, but this in turn will be followed by the decline and dependence of old age and death. To say that humans inhabit bodies that are mortal and corruptible is to say our bodily existence exists within limits. But such limits, Tolle writes, like the identities we create, are illusory, for the

> dense physical structure called the body, which is subject to disease, old age, and death, is not ultimately you. It is a misperception of your essential reality that is beyond birth and death and is due to the limitations of your mind, which, having lost touch with Being, creates the body as evidence of its illusory belief in separation and to justify its state of fear.[1]

The "limitations of your mind" are due to one's failure to recognize that there is a place outside of time—the eternal now—that we can inhabit without fear of corruptibility and death, and where we can be our most true selves. As Tolle has it, we cannot bring our actual, physical bodies with us to this place; our bodies must firstly pass away. Short of death, and partly living in this world, Tolle's answer is that we must disassociate ourselves from our body in order to access this place of Being. For Tolle, this is welcome news, as none of what we leave behind is essential to our true selves, and what is truly essential will be with us in Being.

As for those who identify with their own bodies, or are uncertain as to what their selves might look like separated from bodies, Tolle puts to us the following question:

> When there is nothing to identify with anymore, who are you? When forms around you die or death approaches, your sense of Beingness, of I Am, is freed from its entanglement of form. Spirit is released from its imprisonment in matter. You realize your essential identity is formless as an all-pervasive Presence, of Being prior to all forms, all identifications. You recognize your true consciousness is

---

1. Tolle, *Power of Now*, 116.

consciousness itself, rather than what consciousness had identified with.[2]

For Tolle, the body is a prison that holds captive the spirit of those who identify with it. Such imprisonment is due in great part, as said earlier, to the mortal, corruptible, temporal nature of bodily life. There are other elements of bodily existence that are limiting as well, not the least of which is gender.

Not only is that body located in a particular space, as Edith Stein argued in chapter 1, but the soul is assigned at birth (or conception) to a body that is of a particular gender. As Tolle writes:

> Apart from objects, another basic form of identification is with "my" body. Firstly, the body is male or female, and so the sense of being a man or woman takes up a significant part of most people's sense of self. Gender becomes identity. Identification with gender becomes important at an early age, and it forces you into a role, into conditioned patterns of behavior that affect all aspects of your life, not just sexuality.[3]

I think we can agree with Tolle that such a gendered body determines in large part how one's caregivers will treat us as infants, what they will encourage us to desire, what toys we will be given, and what roles they will assign to us. And, of course all of this comes about unconsciously, thereby increasing its influence. Moreover, such bodies will vary in size, shape, strength, attractiveness, and ability. The way we dress tells others about ourselves in terms of social class, status, occupation, education, and levels of dependence and independence.

It could be argued that there is a connection between the body's influence upon us and its temporality. When we encounter another body for the first time, one of the elements we note quickly, albeit often unconsciously, is the age of the body. Is this a young person or an old person? Is this person my age, or is its age more or less hard to determine. For Tolle, the falseness of the

---

2. Tolle, *New Earth*, 56.
3. Tolle, *New Earth*, 49.

false self is the result of forms—thought forms, historical, material, cultural, bodily, and social forms. And so, if the true self is a self that is beyond form, the body represents a serious obstacle to finding the true self, for the body is difficult to ignore and impossible to relinquish.

In one's effort to transcend this most determinative of forms, Tolle says we should not denigrate the body, a belief and practice in which some religious traditions have engaged. Rather, one should simply learn that "to refrain from identifying with the body doesn't mean that you neglect, despise, or no longer care for it. If it is strong, beautiful, and vigorous, you can enjoy and appreciate those attributes—while they last. You can also improve the body's condition through right nutrition and exercise. If you don't equate the body with who you are, when beauty fades, vigor diminishes, or the body becomes incapacitated, this will not affect your sense of self-worth or identity in any way."[4]

Indeed, the corruption of the physical body is a good thing, for Tolle, as when the body weakens, the "formless dimension, the light of consciousness, can shine forth more easily through the fading form."[5] For some of us, the experience of the corruption of the physical body may be unwelcome news, were it not for the good news that comes with it—that such corruption inspires us to redirect our focus and energy toward Being, and, in doing this, one comes a step closer to becoming one's true self.

Despite previous claims that the body functions as a prison that incarcerates one's spirit, the body for Tolle is a form that is more—not less—easily transcended: "Although body identification is one of the most basic forms of ego, the good news is that it is also the one that you can most go beyond. This is done not by trying to convince yourself that you are not your body, but by shifting your attention from the external form of your body and from thoughts about your body—beautiful, ugly, strong, weak, too fat, too thin, to the feeling of aliveness inside it."[6] In this way

---

4. Tolle, *New Earth*, 51.
5. Tolle, *New Earth*, 51.
6. Tolle, *New Earth*, 52.

A Critique of Tolle's Notion of the Body

Tolle redirects one's attention, and shifts the argument, from the outer-physical body to an "inner body."

Whereas the visible, outer body serves as a temporary vessel to transport one's transcendent, true self through the material world, the invisible, inner body serves as a portal into Being, into "Life Unmanifested," as he puts it. "Through the inner body, you are forever one with God."[7]

Unlike the diminished outer, physical body, the "inner body" is, as Tolle presents it, not a body at all; rather, it is a "life energy" in which one experiences a "global sense of aliveness."[8] As with Being itself, but unlike the outer body, the "inner body does not change with time"[9] which is to say it is eternal. When one gets in touch with one's inner body, the outer body is exposed as a mind-made illusion, allowing the inner body more access through the portal that takes us to formlessness. In this way, just as the rejection of forms began the process of freeing oneself from the prison of the ego, so the demise and decay of the physical body frees the "inner body" from the prison of the physical body. Both cases—mind and body—involve a movement from form to formlessness, from time to timelessness.

Along with serving as a portal to formlessness and Being, one's attention to the aliveness of the "inner body" offers many health benefits to the outer body: it makes one feel lighter, allows one to live longer, increases one's presence, and strengthens one's immune system.[10]

Tolle at times in *The Power of Now* writes that "you are your body," and "do not turn your attention elsewhere in your search for Truth, for it is nowhere else to be found but within your body."[11] Such positive references to "the body" make his message more palatable to a modern audience, who have been exposed to a steady diet of health messaging for decades now, even as these statements

---

7. Tolle, *Power of Now*, 116.
8. Tolle, *New Earth*, 53.
9. Tolle, *Power of Now*, 122.
10. Tolle, *Power of Now*, 123.
11. Tolle, *Power of Now*, 116.

appear contradictory to Tolle's message. But "the Truth" of which Tolle speaks to be found in one's body is not the truth of the physical body, but invariably such references are to the "inner body." If there is something positive to tell us about the outer, physical body, Tolle tells us, it is that its corruptible nature, its limitations, and mortality serves the purpose of redirecting oneself to what really matters, and what is truly real, that being the inner body. In short, the best way to live a longer, healthier life is by connecting with the inner body.

TOLLE AS NEO-PLATONIST

Tolle's philosophy of the body, and indeed to understand Tolle's project in general, is greatly illuminated by the fifth- and fourth-century Greek (or Athenian) philosopher Plato. Reviewing Plato's philosophy allows us to fill out, as it were, the gaps in Tolle's teaching, extending his arguments to their logical conclusion.

It should be noted, however, that Tolle would find this comparison objectionable, for he has argued that his teaching "is not derived from external sources, but from the one true source within, so it contains no theory or speculation."[12] To suggest Tolle's teaching is in the Platonic tradition is at once to invite the response that his is not a "new belief system, a new religion, spiritual ideology, or mythology." Rather, his is a "new consciousness" that promotes a "transcendence of thought, the newfound ability or rising above thought, of realizing a dimension within yourself that is infinitely more vast than thought."[13] Plato's discourse is very similar, describing the practical wisdom he promotes as "rising above" the thinking of ordinary thought, social conventions, religion, and mythology and represents an irreducible "essence" or purity of thought.

Like Tolle, Plato's project is one of empowering his students, of assuming a transcendent god's-eye view from which one can

---

12. Tolle, *Power of Now*, 10.
13. Tolle, *New Earth*, 21–22.

A Critique of Tolle's Notion of the Body

survey all from a place of emotional detachment, stability, and omniscience. Like Tolle, Plato identifies that which corrupts, and that from which one must detach to achieve consciousness with the physical body. Tolle's primary argument against the body is that it exists in time, which is to say it is mortal, and therefore will pass away. Being temporal, Tolle insists there is nothing in the physical body that is essentially us, that which makes us who we are; there is nothing of us in the form of our physical body that will survive death. Plato shares Tolle's view of the body's corruptibility, but goes on to explain that beyond mortality, there are several elements that originate with and are promoted by the body that causes mortals to judge and live falsely in real time: the emotions, passion/desire, and physical appetites.

Two physical appetites that Plato finds most vexing—hunger and sexual desire—are problematic because they disrupt and undermine the intellectual and interpretive dimensions of the soul that are critical of sound judgment, practical reasoning, and living well. One's surrendering to the physical appetites, as Plato sees it, amounts to the creation of a prison in which one incarcerates oneself, in which the prison walls prevent one from seeing the world beyond the self. Passion and desire, like physical appetites, for Plato and Tolle, also distort and limit good perception and judgment and, in so doing, misdirect our action. The bodily elements have this effect because they, firstly, promote dependence on objects outside the self and, secondly, because such objects are inherently unstable. That we desire suggests a need and dependence that is intensified by our pursuit of that which we desire. To desire is to desire an object not in my possession, to experience physical appetites is to experience deprivation, the eventual satisfaction of which brings a temporary stability; to experience emotions is to be destabilized in some way, to have one's equanimity disrupted, and in the end to be vulnerable to moral and intellectual error. Physical health, financial security, sexual satisfaction, and all-around physical satiation are, like the physical body itself, mutable, fragile, subject to chance, loss, and corruption. For Plato, the body is a necessary but impermanent vessel into which the permanent spirit is poured.

Emotions, though more educable than bodily appetite for Tolle and Plato, nevertheless must be monitored closely, lest we fall into "madness." As Martha Nussbaum puts it, "Plato repudiated emotion and appetite as corrupting influences, insisting that correct practical judgments are reached only by encouraging the intellect to go off 'itself by itself,' free from their influence as far as possible. The condition of the person in which [emotion and appetite] lead or guide intellect is given the pejorative name of 'madness,' which is definitionally contrasted with rationality or soundness of judgment."[14]

Tolle, too, speaks of "madness," as we saw in the previous chapter; unlike Plato, however, who associates it with emotion, Tolle associates it with the inner conversations—the "mental noise," as he calls it—that accompanies us in our day-to-day lives.

At this point, adherents to Tolle's teaching would defend him by arguing that Tolle's notion of Being is a no-mind, a non-thinking, and a non-intellectual place that puts Tolle at odds with Plato in this matter regarding the role of the intellect. But this is not the case, I am arguing, as Tolle goes on to say: "The beginning of freedom is the realization that you are not the processing entity—the thinker. Knowing this enables you to observe the entity. The moment you start watching the thinker, a higher level of consciousness becomes active. You then begin to realize that there is a vast realm of intelligence beyond thought, that thought is only a tiny aspect of intelligence."[15]

For Tolle, freedom from thought paradoxically requires a "knowing" that enables one to observe the thinker. Such "knowing" he equates with "consciousness" and "a vast realm of intelligence." In other words, for Tolle, knowing, consciousness, and Being are intertwined in a way that "knowing" is in fact part of "Being." Such an argument, however, invites the question of what the difference between thinking and knowing might be. Plato answers this by

---

14. Nussbaum, *Fragility of Goodness*, 77.
15. Tolle, *Power of Now*, 17.

making a distinction between the thinking of the philosopher and the thinking of the ordinary person in which the thinking of the philosopher is about universals—goodness, truth, and beauty, for example—and the thinking of ordinary humans focuses on the particulars of life—when the next meal will be and the price of gasoline at the pump. Such thinking about transcendence and universals, which for Plato is the thought that counts, comes under various names such as "asceticism," "contemplation," and "spiritual knowledge." In this way, the issue is not between thinking and non-thinking, as Tolle suggests, but between realms of thinking of practical, ordinary, day-to-day thinking, on the one hand, and the higher, other-worldly realm of pure thought, on the other hand. In other words, Tolle's Being, consciousness, and transcendence share many similarities to Plato's concept of pure intellect. Elsewhere Tolle describes thinking as limited because it comes from a singular perspective, and is surpassed by "awareness," which is a form of thinking, but thinking from multiple, indeed all, perspectives at the same time. The enlightened and conscious person enjoys an omniscience—knowing all and seeing all, and thus operates from a place of facts, as opposed to opinions—that Tolle describes in opposition to emotional thinking and "emotional story-making,"[16] which are mere opinions.

Tolle considers the ecology of human emotions as problematic in ways very similar to Plato, who argued that emotions, like human appetites, distort human perception and judgment because they focus our attention on objects in the world that are material and therefore highly mutable and inherently unstable. Like Plato, Tolle associates emotions with the physical body, in which, like the fight-or-flight response of animals to threats in their environment, humans have a fight-or-flight response in our bodies to our thoughts. As with the fight-or-flight response of nonhuman animals, the human animal body also reacts to events in its environment, "but it will be a response to the event seen through the filter of a mental interpretation, the filter of thought, that is to say, through the mental concepts of good and bad, like and dislike, me

16. Tolle, *New Earth*, 135.

and mine."[17] Some of our thoughts are more like reactions, Tolle goes on to write, in that they have an immediacy about them that is unconscious:

> They have their origin in a person's past conditioning, usually from early childhood. "People cannot be trusted" would be an example of such an unconscious assumption in a person whose primordial relationships—that is to say, with parents or siblings—were not supportive and did not inspire trust. Here are a few more unconscious assumptions: "Nobody respects and appreciates me. I need to fight to survive. There is never enough money. Life always lets you down. I don't deserve abundance. I don't deserve love." Unconscious assumptions create emotions in the body which in turn generate mind activity and/or instant reactions. In this way they create your personal reality.[18]

For Tolle, just as thoughts and thinking contribute to the creation of one's false, egoic self, so the emotions that are generated from the body's response to past conditioning contribute to this false self. Emotions cannot be trusted any more than thinking (or "dysfunctional" thinking—a new category Tolle introduces later in *A New Earth* that revises his critique of thinking; that is to say, through the first half of the book, the ego—the false self—is the result of thought and thinking; in time, however, Tolle makes the distinction between thinking and dysfunctional thinking, inviting the question of why he is not promoting "functional thinking"). As Tolle puts it, such thinking is the source of "ego-generated emotions" which are "derived from the mind's identification with external factors which are, of course, unstable and liable to change at any moment."[19]

However, things can go the other way as well, that our thoughts create a bodily emotional response, as we have said, but our emotions then, in turn, inform our thinking, resulting in "a

---

17. Tolle, *New Earth*, 133.
18. Tolle, *New Earth*, 135.
19. Tolle, *New Earth*, 137.

vicious circle between unexamined thoughts and emotions, giving rise to emotional thinking and emotional story-making."[20] Such a notion is not unlike Immanuel Kant's idea of pure reason, the belief that humans can inhabit a pure intellect, unsullied and uncorrupted by experience, physicality, history, culture, and emotion.

By now, it should be clear that a central part of Tolle and Plato's project is to empower humans to purify themselves of "emotional thinking and emotional story-making" so that they might rise above the messiness of the embodied and emotional life to a place of pure Being (for Tolle) and Truth, Goodness, and Beauty (for Plato). Complicating this for Tolle, however, is that the emotions have a cumulative effect, are compounded over time. Such compounding of thoughts and emotions take the form of memories, which in time take on particular themes, which then become stories on which humans base their sense of self, identity, who they are. Another result of such cumulative negative emotions is an "energy field" that we carry with us, what Tolle calls "the pain body."

Not only is the "pain body" the cumulative emotions that one builds up in oneself, but there is a collective pain body that individuals inherit from the familial, ethnic, and national cultures in which they are socialized. As Tolle puts it, "The pain-body, however, is experienced not only by individuals. It also partakes of the suffering of countless humans throughout the history of humanity, which is a history of continuous tribal warfare, of enslavement, pillage, rape, torture, and other forms of violence. The pain still lives in the collective psyche of humanity and is being added to on a daily basis, as you can verify when you watch the news tonight or look at the drama in people's relationships."[21] Presence, or living in the present moment, Tolle goes on to say, is that which over time can release us from history—which includes a history of emotion—and dissolves the power of the pain-body, the result of which is that "your thinking ceases to be clouded by emotion; your present perceptions are no longer distorted by the

---

20. Tolle, *New Earth*, 135.
21. Tolle, *New Earth*, 142–43.

past."[22] Like Plato, Tolle sees emotions akin to the body and its appetites—that which functions like an opaque curtain that clouds our self-understanding, perception, thinking, and prevents us from ascending to a transcendent place of pure consciousness so that we might perceive accurately and judge rightly. Such a transcendent place is a place of peace and security because it affords us a self-sufficiency untroubled by bodily and emotional life. The re-creation of human beings as self-sufficient and trouble-free, so I am arguing, is at the heart of their common projects, something that will be explored in more detail in the chapter 3.

ARISTOTLE'S CRITIQUE OF TOLLE'S NOTIONS OF THE EMOTIONS, DESIRE, APPETITES, AND THE BODY

Unlike Tolle—who argues that emotions, desire, and bodily appetites are obstacles to transcendence and Being, serve as a "prison" of one's own making, and thus prevent good judgment and perception—Aristotle argues that emotions, desire, and bodily appetites play an essential role in human self-understanding and action. With this in mind, he puts forth an account of emotion as necessary for the cultivation of practical wisdom and good judgment. After exposing the corrupting effects of "self-indulgence," Aristotle goes on to say in the first chapter of the *Nicomachean Ethics*, "On the other hand, men deficient in regards to pleasure, who find less delight in them than they should, are scarcely ever found, for such insensitivity is not human. Even the animals discriminate between different kinds of food and enjoy some and not others. If there is someone to whom nothing is pleasant and who does not differentiate one thing from another, he must be anything but a man. There is no name for such a creature, since he is scarcely to be found."[23]

There are three primary ways in which Aristotle claims emotion, desire, and appetites play a constructive role in the development of practical wisdom. The first is the motivational role that

---

22. Tolle, *New Earth*, 162.
23. Aristotle, *Nicomachean Ethics*, 1119a 6–10.

A Critique of Tolle's Notion of the Body

emotions and appetites play, both in one's formation as a child, as well as for adults. As Martha Nussbaum puts it, emotion, desire, and appetites are what push us out into the world in the first place, making us active agents in the making and remaking of the world around us, but then "impelling the person towards more appropriate objects in keeping with his or her evolving conception of the appropriate."[24] Because desires are pliable, they can be directed to objects of desire that are good for us, that for which we have good reason to desire, and discourage us from desiring objects for which one has no good reason to desire.

Emotion, desire, and appetites can play a constructive role in the act of choosing and moral decision making. The employment of "good reasons" for desiring in the process of choosing is not a matter of "stepping back," or "rising above," as Tolle and Plato have it, so that we might assume a position of unbiased, scientific certainty in our choices. Such "stepping back" and "rising above" for Aristotle takes us to a place of generality and abstraction that deprives us of the ability to make good judgments in the first place, for good judgment requires paying attention to the particularities and concreteness of the matters at hand. Having "good reasons" for our choices, or choosing well, for Aristotle, involves proper training of one's emotions and appetites, which in turn leads or guides the intellect in making good choices. Emotion/desire/appetites go back and forth with the intellect, each shaping the other, to form a dynamic that constitutes our character, character being the most fundamental component of human agency for Aristotle. Character for him is what makes for a functioning human being. At the same time, Aristotle has it that emotions—again, well-directed emotions—are that which, in the end, set us most on the action trajectory one takes in any given particular situation. As Nussbaum puts it, "The experienced person confronting a new situation does not attempt to face it with the intellect 'itself by itself.' He or she faces it, instead, with desires informed by deliberation, and deliberation

---

24. Nussbaum, *Fragility of Goodness*, 307.

informed by desire, and responds to it appropriately in both passion and act."[25]

Desire for Aristotle plays a critical role in the development of practical wisdom in that it "marks" items in our experience of the world around us, items to be pursued or items to be avoided. Without desire, the vastness of stimuli, the multitude of objects that surround us at every moment in our day-to-day lives, would overwhelm us, rendering us incapable of action, had it not been for some kind of selectivity in terms of which stimuli to pay attention to, and what to ignore. It is desire, sometimes simple, wishful desire, and sometimes appetitive desire, that narrows the field for us, brings certain elements to our attention, and then invites us to determine whether or not we have good reason to pursue this object of desire, include it in our deliberation before we act. It is not as though we are a blank page starting from scratch with each new situation we find ourselves in. Part of practical wisdom involves reminding ourselves that the person we are, and thus the deliberating we are currently engaged in, is the result of past objects of desire that were realized, rejected, or delayed, and in each case has already contributed to the formation of the selves and intellects that we are.

There is a third way in which emotion, passion, and the appetites play a constructive role in one's growth in practical wisdom. Without the right emotions, for Aristotle, a moral choice can be less than virtuous. As he puts it:

> Virtuous actions are noble and are performed because they are noble. Accordingly, a generous man, too, will give—and give in a correct manner—because that is noble. He will give to the right people, the right amount, at the right time, and do everything else that is implied in correct giving. Moreover, it will give him pleasure to do so, or (at least) no pain. . . . If he gives to the wrong people, or for the wrong motive, and not because it is

---

25. Nussbaum, *Fragility of Goodness*, 308.

noble to give, he will not be called generous but something else.[26]

And so, the person who experiences his or her generosity toward another as painful is deficient in that he or she has the incorrect passional disposition, and thus the generous act is less virtuous; he or she who experiences pleasure in giving is more virtuous because he or she has the correct emotional disposition.

In the former's case, the agent has more moral work to do, in which it is assumed by Aristotle that emotions—including pleasure and pain—are pliable. That is, part of developing a virtuous character is training oneself to experience the appropriate emotions in conjunction with the appropriate actions. In this way one cultivates in oneself the desire to do good, and in time to be good, thereby contributing to the growth of one's good character.

A fourth, but by no means final, aspect to the constructive role the emotions, desires, and appetites play in the development of one's practical wisdom, for Aristotle, is the recognition that the emotions and appetites serve to remind us that we are dependent and insufficient creatures. Aristotle wants us to inhabit a form, the particularly human form, and his notion of practical wisdom is to assist us in flourishing in that project, a project that is positioned over and against the Tolleian project of ascending to an omniscient, detached, impersonal, third-person place. Such a place, Aristotle would argue, is a place that assumes and reinforces an illusion of human self-sufficiency and invulnerability.

For Tolle and Plato the wise person aspires to detachment from the physical body, and likewise aspires to detach from emotion, desire, passion, and appetite, all of which imprison our souls and cloud our consciousness. Such a project is misguided, Aristotle argues, because it constitutes a way of life that does not ring true to our experience. Tolle and Plato, Aristotle would say, put forth a model of wisdom and truth that may be good for immortal and disembodied beings such as spirits, gods, and angels, but it

---

26. Aristotle, *Nicomachean Ethics*, IV 1124–30.

does not characterize, nor is it helpful to, those of us who inhabit and operate in this human and material world.

For Tolle and Plato, the task of excelling in practical wisdom, of which the hallmark is truthful perception and judgment, is one of transcending materiality and bodiliness, so that we might rest in Being. In contrast, for Aristotle, the task of growing in practical wisdom is inhabiting the form, not of Being by itself, but of a *Human* Being. In this way, Aristotle's project of empowering us to excel in practical wisdom is species specific—that species being the *homo sapien*. Aristotle is not interested in an abstract, spiritual "inner body," as Tolle has it; rather, Aristotle is interested in the human body as it plays out as a particular animal species, that of the human animal.

The ideal of the true philosopher for Tolle and Plato is someone who transcends ordinary humanness and, in so doing, the philosopher acquires a self-sufficiency in thought and action. Such self-sufficiency brings with it an ideal of the philosopher that can be described as solitary—a solitude perfectly embodied in the life and personality of the philosopher Socrates (of course presented to us from the point of view and pen of Plato).

In response, Aristotle would say that such a self-sufficiency and solitude obscures and conceals a critical dimension to human animality—that we are dependent animals with needs that must be satisfied through our cooperation with others. On the one hand, Aristotle acknowledges that self-sufficiency is a human good for which we naturally strive. "However," as he puts it, "we define something as self-sufficient not by reference to the 'self' alone. We do not mean a man who lives his life in isolation, but a man who lives with parents, children, a wife, and friends and fellow citizens generally, since man is by nature a social and political being."[27]

This, in many ways, is a signature quality of Aristotle's human animal. While other animals are characterized by flight (such as birds and insects), or strength (such as bears and lions), sheer mass (such as a whale or elephant), or cunning (as in the wasp or the fox), human animal survival and flourishing is accomplished in

---

27. Aristotle, *Nicomachean Ethics*, I 1097b 5–10.

A Critique of Tolle's Notion of the Body

part through practical reasoning, resourcefulness and cooperation with fellow members of their species.

For Aristotle, the appetites of the body, such as hunger and sexual desire, serve to remind us, at the very least, that humans are not self-sufficient beings; rather, from our very beginnings as infants, and in the decline of old age, human creatureliness is defined by neediness and dependence, and thus are driven to create forms of interdependence.

MACINTYRE'S ACKNOWLEDGED DEPENDENCE

Contemporary philosopher Alasdair MacIntyre spells out the consequences of this failure to see human existence as a this-worldly, particular, and animal/species existence, and seeks to revitalize Aristotle's argument that human dependence and animal bodiliness ought to play a central role in human self-understanding.

At the beginning of his book *Dependent Rational Animals*, MacIntyre brings to our attention the fact that the vast majority of writing in moral philosophy has been done from the point of view of independent, rational agents by whom "only passing references to human vulnerability and affliction and to the connections between them and our dependence on others"[28] are made. And so, when the ill, injured, and disabled are brought up, they are treated by moral philosophers as subjects of charity for able-bodied, independent adults who are presented as rational, untroubled, and self-sufficient. The result, MacIntyre argues, is a marked delineation between "us" and "them," between the unafflicted and the afflicted, in such a way that deprives us—the unafflicted—of the skills to recognize that we can fall prey to illness, injury, and disability at any time. This inability to see ourselves as vulnerable to illness, injury, and affliction, gives us a false sense of security, a sense of invulnerability, and independence.

One possible remedy for this is to acknowledge that this false sense of invulnerability and self-sufficiency is a deeply ingrained

---

28. MacIntyre, *Dependent Rational Animals*, 1.

cultural habit that is not easily undone. A second step is to identify the assumptions that undergird these habits, a primary one being the extent to which "we conceive of ourselves, and imagine ourselves as other than animal, as exempt from the hazardous condition of 'mere' animality."[29]

It is interesting how, as human animals, we view undomesticated, nonhuman animals as living a precarious existence. We intuitively sense that things can go wrong for them at any time. A fawn gets tangled in a fence, our chickens are killed by a fox, a crow carcass is found in a field, an owl's leg is in a trap. But the sense of a precarious existence does not beset modern humans in the same way as non-domesticated, nonhuman animal life. This is due, MacIntyre argues, in part to a psychological distance humans maintain between ourselves and nonhuman animals. The sense that humans are somehow excepted from such vulnerabilities is due, in part, to the belief that "non-human animals cannot have thoughts, beliefs, or reasons for action." This assumption, MacIntyre goes on to say, "may seem to provide grounds for the belief that our rationality as thinking beings is somehow independent of our animality. We become forgetful of our bodies and of how our thinking is the thinking of one species of animal."[30]

The place to which MacIntyre seeks to bring us requires several steps. The first step is to help human animals understand the substance and extent to which our human animal thinking has evolved, building upon nonhuman animal thinking. The next step is to extend this so that we increase our capacity as "independent rational agents."[31] But this brings with it an increase in our understanding of the virtues we need "if we are to confront and respond to vulnerability and disability both in ourselves and in others."[32] To increase our ability to survive and even flourish in our bodily, animal existence, means that we must be mindful of the vulnerability that comes with it; at the same time to survive and

---

29. MacIntyre, *Dependent Rational Animals*, 4.
30. MacIntyre, *Dependent Rational Animals*, 5.
31. MacIntyre, *Dependent Rational Animals*, 5.
32. MacIntyre, *Dependent Rational Animals*, 5.

A Critique of Tolle's Notion of the Body

flourish means that we must develop skills so that we might better navigate the complexities of our environment. Such skillfulness in identifying goals, working with others, understanding the risks, and executing a plan of action requires a kind of independence of mind. At the same time, we acknowledge our dependence on those who contributed to the skills we have acquired over time, and the condition of dependence we may at any time experience were we to be injured, become ill, or suffer affliction. The virtues of independent rational animals, and the virtues of the acknowledged dependent rational animal are one and the same, MacIntyre says. This is due in part because we cannot become independent rational agents without acknowledging our bodily vulnerability and therefore dependence upon others, both intellectually and practically. And so, whereas Tolle and Plato promote a notion of transcendence beyond time and physicality—the "rise above" position we talked about earlier—MacIntyre ascribes a notion of deepening our temporality and animality from which our human rationality has evolved but never transcended. Animality brings with it limitations that human animals mitigated, "but in doing so have never separated ourselves entirely from what we share with them. Indeed our ability to transcend those limitations depends in part upon certain of those animal characteristics, among them the nature of our identity."[33]

What we share with nonhuman animals in terms of identity is a bodily identity, by which MacIntyre means that our bodies are continuous with other bodies, such that when one body experiences injury, illness, and affliction, the relationships of dependence and independence with other bodies changes. In this way, the privileged place of independent rational agency needs to be "accompanied by what I shall call the virtues of acknowledged dependence."[34]

To understand independent rational agency and acknowledged dependence, MacIntyre puts forth a line of thinking that begins with flourishing. And to keep his line of thinking grounded

33. MacIntyre, *Dependent Rational Animals*, 8.
34. MacIntyre, *Dependent Rational Animals*, 8.

within time and human and nonhuman nature—in contrast to Tolle's outside of time and nature, i.e., the physical body—MacIntyre explores flourishing firstly in dolphin social life and then in human social life.

To understand what flourishing in dolphin life looks like, we must have some knowledge of dolphin life structure, of which MacIntyre writes, "Dolphins live together in groups or herds with well-defined social structures. Although we do not yet understand very much about the sequence of whistles and squeals that they utter, it is clear that they excel at vocal learning and communicate with one another in a variety of ways. They form different types of social bonds and exhibit affections and passions. They are subject to fear and to stress. They are purposeful, they are playful, and they engage purposefully in play."[35]

Non-domesticated animal life is precarious in general, and dolphin life is no exception. Dolphin herds are susceptible to hunger, privation, disease, injury, and harm from predators, both human and nonhuman. While some dolphin herds manage to thrive, others struggle and die. But of those that thrive, they "flourish only because they have learned how to achieve their goals through strategies concerted with other members of the different groups to which they belong or which they encounter."[36]

The goals of a herd of dolphins are multiple, all of which are directed to the common good, that being the appropriation of resources and social interaction such as play and hunting that promotes its flourishing. For the herd to achieve the goal of successful hunting, it must practice a variety of skills that involve communication, strategy, and coordination.

As with humans, the young are dependent upon the herd for their survival. They are fed regardless of their ability to hunt. At the same time, the independent reasoning dolphins devote time and resources to the education of dependent dolphins so that, in time, the young might transition to independent-functioning dolphins who can contribute to the herd as hunters. The degree to which the

---

35. MacIntyre, *Dependent Rational Animals*, 21.
36. MacIntyre, *Dependent Rational Animals*, 23.

herd flourishes or diminishes depends in great part upon this dynamic of dependence to independence, in terms of an individual dolphin's relationship to the herd.

As has been shown with the dolphin community, the goals of individuals within a community are to meet the needs of the community. It is possible that some human animals, with enough resources and good health, may for a while be self-sufficient. But by and large in order to flourish, human animals need to live in community. The needs of a plant community—soil which is stable and not prone to erosion, light, fertility, and moisture—must be provided and amended for it to flourish; the needs of an animal-community such as dolphins are freedom from predators, the existence of sustainable habitat, food supply, relatively low levels of water toxicity—needs that, when met, allow the herd and all individuals in the herd, to flourish. Though the needs for a human community to flourish may differ in species, they do not differ in kind with plant and animal life. The *needs* of which we speak here are, as MacIntyre writes, "one and the same concept of needs that find similar broad application. What a plant or animal needs is what it needs to flourish qua member of a particular species. And what it needs to flourish is to develop the distinctive powers that it possesses qua member of that species."[37]

Though the objects upon which needs are based may differ from species to species, the status of need and dependence in human life is the same as that of animal life and plant life. To think of the basic conditions for human flourishing, one can begin with—and perhaps even end with—thinking of the needs related to the having and caring for children. Such things as healthy food and clean water, safe and secure living spaces, access to health care, minimal levels of financial security, access to good education. With this of course comes a host of other goods—individual goods, to be sure, but such individual goods cannot be separated from both public and common goods, as the hope is the child will continue to benefit from, and contribute to, the larger group. The deliberation over which of these goals qualify as needs and whose

---

37. MacIntyre, *Dependent Rational Animals*, 64.

responsibility it is to provide for them at what level is a political activity that we will not get into. The point is to think about conditions that contribute to human flourishing as the same conditions that allow for the successful having and caring for children.

While Aristotle's project is one of developing a kind of practical wisdom that is designed to make possible and promote human flourishing, Tolle's project is one of promoting awareness, consciousness and "spiritual transformation." What Tolle offers is a theory of self-sufficiency and transcendence from physical lack that is made possible through a focus and relocation of the embodied self to a place of pure Being—a theory, so I am arguing, that diminishes temporality, physicality and, with it, and proper understanding of human dependency. It does so at great cost to a rightful recognition of what is needed to flourish as human individuals and communities.

To sum up, this critique of Tolle's teachings of the body is threefold. Firstly, the talk of "spiritual transformation" denies, or at least fails in its accounting of, the species-specific aspects of human physicality, identity, and sociality. With this depreciation of one's physical body, for Tolle, comes redirecting of one's attention to one's "inner body" where we take up an existence as disembodied, transcendent, and immaterial Beings. Tolle's teaching distorts and undermines our efforts to live in accord with our embodied, terrestrial nature by presenting physical vulnerability and dependency as symptoms of lack and deficiency that are to be overcome through a depreciation of social and public forms of life. Secondly, recognizing one's animal condition provides us with a point of view that promotes three critical skills: it allows one to recognize human physical and psychological vulnerability; this in turn allows us to recognize that we, like the disabled, ill, and injured, are vulnerable to these same afflictions. When such affliction happens, we will be in need of the care of others. And lastly, viewing need and dependency as essential to human life, as something to be embraced, allows us, when we enjoy a certain degree of rational and physical independence, to care for those in a state of dependence. Time and physicality should not be viewed as constraints to be transcended, as Tolle has it, but as the conditions for our existence within which human and nonhuman animal life flourishes, or at least must learn to flourish. Like animal life, human animal life is precarious, but within its unpredictability, we continue to develop the skills of resourcefulness and cooperation that make for the conditions for human flourishing. Indeed, it could be said that such resourcefulness, as well as a rationality that has transcended but never superseded our animality, is the hallmark of humanness. Resourcefulness and rationality are in great part that which separates us from the divine life of gods and angels who are self-sufficient, on the one hand, and other creatures, like plants in the earth, whose existence is more at the mercy of the earth on the other hand.

3

Tolle's Disregard for the Particular

IN THE CHAPTER 2 we looked at a central theme in Tolle's teaching regarding the movement from the particular physical, or "outer" body, to the universal "inner body." This is just one of many examples of the way in which Tolle diminishes that which is particular—actions, objects, beliefs—and promotes categories that are abstract and universal. In this chapter we will look at other aspects of human life in which he shifts our attention from the particular, concrete, and earthly view, and the problems that arise from doing this, according to Aristotle.

Tolle consistently reminds us of the body's corruptibility and the precarious nature of bodily existence. There is an impermanence and dependence that comes with bodily life, one that forces us to appropriate human and material resources to preserve and sustain us, and these resources themselves bring with them their own instability, and so do not entirely eliminate our vulnerability. An example is coupling. Part of marriage or partnering can be viewed as a social form designed to increase our security against the kinds of misfortune that can afflict. But such coupling is often based upon romantic love, itself an unpredictable and unstable thing. So, not only is the support one would hope for in times of injury and affliction an unstable thing, but the criterion for getting us together and keeping us together is also unstable. In short, human life is a precarious business, fraught with instability and uncertainty.

Tolle calls that which is subject to change in human life "forms." These include not only physical forms, such as the body, but emotional and thinking forms as well. Thought forms include religious and political beliefs, as well as ideologies of any kind. His talk of forms also includes emotional forms, such as romantic love, pleasure, grief, fear and anxiety, or memories and the identities upon which they are based.

Likewise, Tolle argues, as we dispossess ourselves of the externalities and physical forms that surround us—possessions, children or spouses, social positions, physicality, recognition—we increase in consciousness and self-knowledge. Those objects and forms that give us a sense of self are the same things that can be taken away, and sometimes taken abruptly, and to no fault of our own, leaving us diminished. For some, however, the loss of externalities can bring a "sense of Presence, a deep peace and serenity and complete freedom from fear."[1] It is then that "you realize your essential identity as formless, as an all-pervasive Presence, of Being prior to all forms, all identifications. You realize your true identity as consciousness itself, rather than what consciousness had identified with."[2]

The forms of which Tolle speaks are made up of objects, beliefs, and emotions that humans identify with or use in concrete, particular ways. Examples include that chair, your anger, my belief in justice. And so there is that which is particular, but there is that which is universal—that which transcends particular beliefs, emotions, and objects in our world. That which is universal includes such things as life, presence, Being, and consciousness. The heavens are transcendent and universal; the plot of land I call my front yard is made of matter, and is particular. In this way, when Tolle speaks of forms, he speaks of particularities. When he speaks

1. Tolle, *New Earth*, 56.
2. Tolle, *New Earth*, 56–57.

of the tendency of humans to identify with form, he is speaking of an identification with particularity (in contrast to that which is transcendent and universal).

Tolle teaches that one's identification with form—that is, with particular beliefs, persons, objects, ideas, emotions—is the work of, and serves to inflate, the ego. And the ego, that which identifies with forms and particularities, has the effect of exacerbating the delusion of one's false self. On the other hand, becoming aware of the transcendent and universal elements of Being, consciousness, and presence allows one to discover one's true self, one's true identity. This movement from that which is particular in one's life to that which is universal is a major theme in Tolle's teaching.

Examples of the movement from the particular to the universal are replete in Tolle's books *The Power of Now* and *A New Earth*. We have already looked at an example of the movement from one's particular physical, or "outer," body, to the universal and "inner body." Other examples of the particular/universal dynamic include mind-made beliefs/consciousness, emotional story-telling/Truth, thoughts/awareness, ego/Presence, temporal/eternal, from accident/essence, the prison of matter/freedom of the spirit, outer purpose/inner purpose. In each case, the particular, and the form that it takes, is unstable and impermanent. At the same time such particularities hold up the possibility of moving us toward that which is universal—transcendence, enlightenment, presence, and Being.

The case of "purpose" provides us with another example of Tolle's methods: there is always that which is under the category of "outer purpose"—raising children, paying off a mortgage, keeping the lawn mowed—which Tolle thinks of as instrumental, practical, busy work of a sort. But then there is one's "inner purpose"—that which is universal, pure, stable, and unchanging. "Outer purpose" for Tolle is particular, and "inner purpose" is universal in which there is a back-and-forth between the two. One example of outer purpose Tolle gives is the caring for children, of which he asks,

> What happens to that meaning when they don't need you and perhaps don't even listen to you anymore? If

TOLLE'S DISREGARD FOR THE PARTICULAR

helping others gives meaning to your life, you depend on others being worse off than yourself so that your life can continue to be meaningful and you can feel good about yourself.... I am not saying here that helping others, caring for your children, or striving for excellence in whatever field, are not worthwhile things to do. For many people, they are an important part of their outer purpose, but outer purpose alone is always relative, unstable, and impermanent.[3]

The particular/universal back-and-forth is a mainstay in Plato's philosophy as well, very similar to Tolle's project. However, Plato's use of language is the inverse of Tolle's. Plato uses the word *form* in the way Tolle's uses the word *formlessness*, by which Plato means that which is unchanging, and that which exists as the perfect ideal of the particular objects on this earth that reflect it.

That which is formless for Plato are forms that exist behind, below, or above the world of matter, images, and human experience. The forms, for Plato, are what is really real, that which can be trusted as immutable, invulnerable to corruption, and timeless. For both Tolle and Plato, that which is particular to human beings and their experience is unstable, illusory, impermanent, and temporal; as a result, human identification with such particulars brings with it frustration and suffering; that which is universal, formless, transcendent, and timeless is incorruptible and the source of peace and freedom from suffering.

TOLLE AND PLATO ON ONENESS

Before we engage Aristotle in his critique of Plato (and, de facto, Tolle) it will be helpful to understand Tolle and Plato's arguments for a oneness and singularity to reality, which works closely with their idea of universality. For Tolle and Plato, one's identification with the many particulars that are part and parcel of one's life—goals, aspirations, purposes, loves, attachments, roles, objects, causes— is the cause of separation, division, and conflict, both

3. Tolle, *New Earth*, 263–64.

internally within each human subject, and externally for society as a whole. And it is the human "ego," for Tolle, that is both the cause and the result of identification with forms. As Tolle put it, "The content of the ego varies from person to person, but in every ego the same structure operates.... They live on identification and separation."[4]

How is it that identification creates separation? As Tolle puts it, and as we've said before, the objects with which we identify are unstable and fleeting, and thus cause the ego to double down, as it were, in its project of acquiring and identifying with objects, both material and ethereal, so as to reinforce one's sense of self. Like the hoarder, the ego can never surround itself with enough objects to feel secure. Indeed, the more it acquires, the more it wants.

The corrective to the human experience of separation and conflict, and the suffering that ensues, for Tolle and Plato, is the promotion of a philosophy, practical wisdom, or system of knowledge, of oneness and singularity which holds the promise of a peaceful, enlightened, and untroubled life, both individually and socially. As Tolle puts it,

> Ego is no more than this: identification with form, which primarily means thought forms. If evil has any reality—and it has a relative, not absolute reality—this is also its definition: complete identification with form—physical form, thought forms, emotional forms. This results in a total unawareness of my connectedness with the whole, my intrinsic oneness with every "other" as well as with the Source. This forgetfulness is original sin, suffering, delusion. When this delusion of utter separateness underlies and governs whatever I think, say, and do, what kind of world do I create?[5]

As Tolle puts it, "Each thing has Beingness, [each thing] is a temporary form that has its origin within the formless one life, the source of all things, all bodies, all forms."[6] Whereas the result of partici-

---

4. Tolle, *New Earth*, 60.
5. Tolle, *New Earth*, 22.
6. Tolle, *New Earth*, 37.

pating in Being is peace, the result of existing outside of Being is a fear of "otherness"—an experience of an "other" as a threat or rival, something that exists as a possible source of conflict and affliction. For this reason Tolle is careful not to give "evil" equal standing with the formlessness of Being that he has been promoting. To do so would be to suggest that evil is outside of Being, enjoys an existence independent of Being, for if evil is not contained within Being, then the universal is no longer a universal; rather it would exist as a multiform, plural reality. And so to make the idea of universality (that which contains everything and excludes nothing) to work, Tolle argues that evil is not self-sufficient, cannot exist on its own—is not an "absolute" reality, but is "relative," which is to say, is dependent upon Being.

Plato puts forth an account of oneness, singleness, and universality that is very similar to Tolle's account, an account that plays an important role in the kind of practical wisdom that the citizens of his Republic are to practice. It is a notion of oneness that begins with Plato's idea of the forms, which he presents most thoroughly in Book X of *The Republic* through a dialogue between Socrates and Glaucon, Plato's brother. Socrates makes his case for a metaphysics of oneness by asking Glaucon to imagine three "species" of beds: one bed is made by God that exists but is spiritual, as it were; a second bed is made by a bed maker, or joiner; and a third bed is made by a painter, which is to say is a painting of a bed (presumably the bed made by the joiner). The bed made by God is not a particular bed; it is not a bed that one can actually sleep in, but is pure bed, bed essence, or Bedness, one could say. It is the ideal form of bed. Glaucon so far agrees that such pure Bedness exists. Socrates then asks Glaucon, "But what as to the joiner? Is not he a workman of the bed?" to which Glaucon says indeed he is the workman of the bed. Socrates then asks if the painter, too, is the workman and maker of such a work, to which Glaucon answers that the painter is decidedly not a maker of a bed, but "as it appears to me, we may most reasonably call him, the imitator of these we call the workman of."[7]

7. Plato, *Republic*, 597d.

Socrates goes on to argue that the painter is unlike the joiner in that he or she is derivative—is deriving the painting from the appearances of particular bed, and thus how the bed appears in its particular colors, angles, shades and textures as they appear to the painter. In this way, the painting is an imitation of the bed, and not the bed itself. But then again, Plato goes on to argue that the bed maker too is an imitator of the form of the bed, the bed that was made by God and exists in nature. As Socrates says of Glaucon, "you call him the imitator who makes what is generated the third from nature."[8]

So there are three species of beds in Plato's scheme: the universal, pure bed itself, made by God and existing in nature; the particular bed made by the joiner, which is an imitation of the universal bed made by God; and the purely imitative bed painted by the painter, and painted from the appearance of the particular bed made by the joiner. In this way, Plato argues the bed maker's bed is an imitation once removed from the pure bed; the painter's bed is an imitation of an imitation that doubly depends upon the Form of the bed in order to have any resemblance to a bed. Thus there is a oneness that exists in terms of beds in that there is only one pure, true, and universal bed, the bed made by God that exists as a Form. Needless to say, the pure Form of the bed is good and true for Plato; the imitative bed of the joiner is deficient, and the painting of the joiner's bed is illusory, pure imitation, and therefore base.

Elsewhere in the *Phaedo*, Plato makes a similar case for Beauty when he asks, "If there is anything beautiful besides Beauty itself, it is beautiful for no other reason than that it shares in that Beauty.... Nothing else makes it beautiful other than the presence of, or the sharing in, or however you may describe its relationship to that Beauty we mentioned, for I will not insist on the precise nature of the relationship, but that all things are made beautiful by beauty."[9] Just as particular beautiful objects—a painting, a sculpture, a landscape—derive their beauty by participating in the Form, Beauty, for Plato the painting of the bed derives its bed

---

8. Plato, *Republic*, 597e.
9. Plato, *Phaedo*, 100c–d.

quality from participating in the Form, Bedness. Both the sculpture and the painting of the bed are derivative, that is, both derive their degree of realness from the degree of closeness to the pure Form of Beauty or Bedness.

As with Tolle, there is a notion of oneness that is promoted here by Plato. However a question is invited in terms of Plato that he does not really answer: if oneness is what we're striving for, is there and, if so, what is the oneness that unifies or contains the Beauty and Bedness of which Plato speaks? In other words, is Being the Form of all forms? Plato refers to this, but does not answer it directly in *The Republic*, when he has Socrates ask Glaucon, "Did you not indeed say, just now, that he [the bed maker] does not make the Form which we say exists, which is bed, but a particular bed? I said so indeed. If he does not make that which is, he does not make real being, but some such thing as being, but not being itself; but if anyone should say, that the work of a bed maker, or of any other handicraft, were real being, he would seem not to say true."[10]

The "real being" of which Plato speaks in this passage, and the "Being" of which Tolle speaks, I am arguing, are indistinguishable from each other. Just as the bed maker makes a particular bed, which is not therefore a "real bed," in Plato's scheme of things, for a "real bed" is a bed that exists in "real being"—"real being" for Plato, being the ultimate final true and real that unifies, universalizes, and contains not only all particular objects, but the other forms such as Beauty and bedness.

PARTICULARITY AND UNIVERSALITY: ARISTOTLE'S CRITIQUE OF PLATO AND TOLLE

Tolle and Plato are engaged in a project that has it that the world of particularities is impermanent, unstable, temporal, and therefore illusory; as a corrective, their project is one that redirects our focus from how things appear to us in our day-to-day lives, to essences

10. Plato, *Republic*, 597a.

that are pure, timeless, uncorrupted, and real. For Tolle and Plato, such appearances as x, y, z are, like the painting of the bed, at best poor (to one degree or another) imitations, and at worst are deceptions. To put stock in the appearance of social, emotional, and thought forms, as Tolle puts it, is to be deluded in one's perception of reality. Indeed, the very word "appearance" brings with it the sense that things are not as they seem, that they exist in appearance only, but not in fact. As Tolle puts it, "Nothing is what it seems to be. The world that you create and see through the egoic mind may seem a very imperfect place, even a vale of tears. But whatever you perceive is only a kind of symbol, like an image in a dream."[11]

Against Plato and Tolle's emphasis of universals, and central to the practical wisdom project of Aristotle, is an argument that appearances—indeed, as with all particularities—should be the starting place for human engagement with the world. As he puts it in Book VI of the *Nicomachean Ethics* regarding what makes for human intelligence, "For it is particular facts that form the starting points or principles for [our knowledge of] the goal of action: universals arise out of particulars. Hence one must have perception of particular facts, and this perception is intelligence."[12]

In saying that intelligence begins with perception of particular facts, Aristotle is not speaking of "facts" in the way Tolle speaks of facts. Tolle has it that "every ego confuses opinions with viewpoints and facts. . . . Every ego is a master of selective perception and distorted interpretation. Only through awareness—not through thinking—can you differentiate between fact and opinion."[13] Tolle's idea of facts is much like the somewhat misunderstood notion of scientific facts in which inquiry begins with the collection of raw and uninterpreted data, which is then mined for patterns and connections, from which the scientist's hypothesis are generated, to eventually be corroborated or not by one's fellow scientists. Such "raw data" is viewed as pure, neutral, uninterpreted, and uncorrupted by human purposes.

11. Tolle, *Power of Now*, 199.
12. Aristotle, *Nicomachean Ethics*, 1143b.
13. Tolle, *New Earth*, 68–69.

Tolle's Disregard for the Particular

In contrast, when Aristotle speaks of "perception of particular facts," he is inclusive of human experience of the objects or "facts" of the matter. He is not interested in a Platonic world of a presumed "raw data" (which is not unlike the Forms) because it is unclear what that mean to us humans as it exists outside of experience. Aristotle's frequent use of the word "perception" suggests a notion that recognizes a dynamic between the perceiver and the object perceived, a dynamic that dispels the idea that objects and beliefs operate like the Platonic Forms. For our purposes, the word "appearances" captures this phenomenon; to say Aristotle gives priority to appearances is to say he gives priority to human experience of particular objects, beliefs, and actions. Tolle, on the other hand, views "appearances" as that which, by definition, lacks in reliability, as far as truth is concerned. "Appearances" brings with it a sense of unreliability insofar as the word suggests that humans bring something to their encounter. For Aristotle, the human experience of things in this world as captured in the word "appearances" does not render them unreliable in what they communicate; rather, the experience we bring to our encounter with appearances, Aristotle says, makes them real, meaningful, and useful to us. Tolle and Plato, on the other hand, give priority to grand theories, abstractions, generalities—all of which are embodied in the word "universal." Who, then, can know and transmit to us what is "fact" and true in Tolle's scheme of things? The answer is the enlightened one, the one who is off by himself, looking from above, or from the outside, not at appearances (from which we can only draw opinions) but at the objects themselves, as they are in their unmitigated essence. Tolle sees himself as that person, and those who subscribe to his teaching can do the same.

This is not to say that Aristotle excludes that which is general and universal from his teaching. He argues that, while general statements have a place in summarizing rules or allowing us to expand the range of application of particulars, general statements are not enough, "For in a discussion of moral actions, although general statements have a wider range of application, statements on particular points have more truth in them: actions are concerned with particulars and our statements must harmonize with them."[14] The general rules, he says, are helpful in expanding the area of application of what we know, but cannot function as a shorthand substitute for the knowledge and experience that come from working with particulars. This is certainly the case in ethics, but even in the sciences, such as medicine, an awareness of the dynamics between particulars and general rules (or universals) is critical. As Aristotle says in the *Nicomachean Ethics*:

> But a physician, a physical trainer, or any other such person can take the care in a particular case when he knows the general rules, that is, when he knows what is good for everyone or what is good for a particular kind of person; for the sciences are said to be, and actually are, concerned with what is common to particular cases. Of course, there is probably nothing to prevent even a person with no scientific knowledge from taking good care in a particular case, if he has accurately observed by experience what happens in a particular case.[15]

In this way what is general knowledge, or universal, is that which is common to particular cases, in which the good physician "accurately" observes the particulars of medicine using cases from the past in one's training and then generalizes it enough so as to transfer that knowledge of particulars to other cases. For example, if a patient arrives displaying symptoms of a stroke, a physician recognizes the particulars of this case by its similarities with other particular cases. At the same time, the physician was taught in medical school from medical books the general conditions of strokes, a general rule that came from doctors who, upon observing particulars, created a general category of "stroke" so as to teach new doctors. Aristotle sums up this dynamic by saying that "it is particular facts that form the starting points or principles for [our knowledge of] the goal of action: universals arise out of

---

14. Aristotle, *Nicomachean Ethics*, 1107a 30–31.
15. Aristotle, *Nicomachean Ethics*, 1180b 12–16.

particulars. Hence one must have perception of particular facts, and this perception is intelligence."[16]

Universals arise out of particulars, Aristotle has it, and not the other way around, as Tolle and Plato have it, in which particulars are recognized and framed after the universal has been clearly established. Tolle's talk of essences and everything emanating from Oneness, and Plato's talk of the forms, are systems of practical wisdom very much at odds with the bold claim that "particular points have more truth in them," according to Aristotle. For Plato (and, by implication, Tolle), as Nussbaum puts it,

> universal rules are themselves the ultimate authorities against which the correctness of particular decisions is to be assessed. As the aspiring Platonic philosopher scrutinizes the particular to see the universal features it exemplifies, and considers it ethically relevant only insofar as it falls under the general form, so the aspiring person of practical wisdom will seek to bring a new case under the rule, regarding its concrete features as ethically salient only insofar as they are instances of the universal.[17]

An example of this is Tolle's retelling of the myth of Narcissus, as we saw in chapter 1. In the myth as it is presented to us, Narcissus sees his reflection in a pond and falls in love with it, to the extent that he is unable to disengage from his gaze. Tolle tells the story of Narcissus as one who engages with, not his reflection in the pond, but the reflection of other people who tell him who he is. In terms of the logic of the two versions, falling in love with oneself, or one's image, at any rate, is not the same thing as other people telling you who you are. So Tolle's (mis)reading of the myth is due to his imposing his truth or universal on the particulars of the story, a truth that says the great error of humanity is to allow particular forms, in this case a social form of other people, to define oneself.

Aristotle has it that humans intuitively operate out of a doctrine of appearances, a belief he develops, refines, and employs

16. Aristotle, *Nicomachean Ethics*, 1143b 2–3.
17. Nussbaum, *Fragility of Goodness*, 299–300.

in his work in biology, metaphysics, and moral philosophy. This is another of Aristotle's poignant critiques of Plato and, de facto, Tolle. It is a conviction that makes a claim upon many of us modern people as well—we who, on the one hand, go about our daily lives operating on the assumption that appearances are valid and can be trusted but, when challenged on a philosophical level, are prone to express a suspicion of appearances and look for some truth behind, under, within, or beyond the appearances. Aristotle's project is one of empowering us to embrace and practice the appearances-method intentionally.

And so, how is it that appearances work in terms of Aristotle's methods? For starters, he uses this method in his moral philosophy, which we will look at more closely later, but in his scientific methods as well, such as what he said about the training of physicians. He uses the appearance method, and explains it in more detail in his metaphysics (in terms of his reflections on particulars and universals). In terms of the practical wisdom, or ethics, as we have been discussing, his method of appearances begins, not with an alleged "raw data" of uninterpreted facts, but with phenomena in the world around us to which beliefs, interpretations, and values have already been ascribed. In other words, the language we use to discuss, for example, moral virtue and vice in relation to pleasure, brings with it certain value assumptions and beliefs. Such cultural assumptions that inform the very language we use to speak of (in the case, again) pleasure are not viewed by Aristotle as something that distorts and prejudices us in our understanding of such phenomena, but are part and parcel of what it means to operate as humans within a particular human community. As Nussbaum astutely observes, "To set down the phainomena [phenomena] is not to look for belief-free facts, but to record our usage and the structure of thought and belief which usage displays."[18] In other words, Aristotle's method of appearances has it that we start with what is conventionally said about particular phenomena, as it appears to us, and attend to the "structure of thought and belief," that it brings with it. Such human "perception" allows him to say

---

18. Nussbaum, *Fragility of Goodness*, 244.

something concrete about the phenomena, to speak from and to members of our particular species so that we might understand and incorporate such appearances within the limits of our understanding of practical wisdom.

There are three steps to Aristotle's belief in the priority of appearances. To illustrate them, I will use Aristotle's reflections on anger in Book IV of the *Nicomachean Ethics*, in which he surveys an array of Greek attitudes regarding anger, the first of which is that those who fail to experience anger are viewed as morally deficient: "For those who do not show anger at things that ought to arouse anger are regarded as fools. . . . Such people seem to have no feelings, not even for pain; they do not seem to rise to their own defense, since they do not show anger; but to let one's character be smeared and to put up with insults from those near and dear to him is slavish."[19] From there he comments on anger as manifested in those who are "sullen," "short tempered," "choleric," and "bad tempered," thereby illustrating the variation and complexity of anger, all of which suggests, he writes, that "it is not easy to determine in what manner, with what person, on what occasion, and for how long a time one ought to be angry, and at what point good action ends and wrong action begins."[20]

Having gathered various phenomena regarding anger, Nussbaum writes Aristotle's method of appearances has it that we must

> set out the puzzles or dilemmas with which they confront us. The phainomena [phenomena] present us with a confused array, often with direct contradiction. They reflect our disagreements and ambivalences. The first step, therefore, is to bring conflicting opinions to the surface and set them out clearly, marshalling the considerations for and against each side, showing how the adoption of a certain side on one issue would affect our position on others.[21]

---

19. Aristotle, *Nicomachean Ethics*, 1126a 4–7.
20. Aristotle, *Nicomachean Ethics*, 1126a 31–35.
21. Nussbaum, *Fragility of Goodness*, 246.

Unlike other disciplines, Aristotle has it that ethics cannot be done with the same kind of precision and certainty as the sciences, but nevertheless things can be said, claims can be made, and conclusions can be drawn. In the case of anger, and having brought such various phenomena to the surface and worked through them, we find Aristotle being a bit less prescriptive, in terms of conclusiveness, than on other topics, for, as he puts it, "sometimes we praise those who are deficient in anger and call them gentle, and sometimes we praise the angry as manly and regard them as capable of ruling."[22] And so, on the one hand, in some cases lack of anger is praiseworthy, and in other cases an abundance of anger is regarded as praiseworthy, such as with someone who might rule. Aristotle tries to resolve this tension by concluding that

> it is not easy to give a formula how far and in what manner a man may stray before he deserves blame, for the decision depends upon the particular circumstance and on our (moral) sense. But this much is clear: what deserves praise is the median characteristic that makes us show anger at the right people, at the right occasions, in the right manner, and so forth, while the extremes and deficiencies deserve blame: slight blame for small deviations, more blame for more deviations, and very severe blame for very great deviations. Thus it is clear that we must hold fast to the median characteristic.[23]

This second step of organizing, revising, realigning, expelling various perceptions can be a complicated business, is something learned slowly and sometimes painfully, but is central to the project of becoming a good person, a competent practitioner of practical wisdom. For Aristotle, the desire for consistency of the many elements regarding, in this case, anger—which is brought about through the recognition and resolution of contradictions—is simply part of human nature. As Nussbaum puts it, "The profound natural desire to bring the matter of life into a perspicuous order will not be satisfied, he believes, as long as there is contradiction.

---

22. Aristotle, *Nicomachean Ethics*, 1126b.
23. Aristotle, *Nicomachean Ethics*, 1126b 1–9.

Tolle's Disregard for the Particular

Our deepest intellectual commitment [as we shall explore in more detail in the chapter 5] is to the principle of non-contradiction, the most basic of all our shared beliefs. The method of appearance-saving therefor demands that we press for consistency."[24]

Some might say at this point on the topic of anger that Aristotle has balked, as it were, defaulting to a kind of situational ethics, a "let-the-individual-decide" conclusion, or lack thereof. But this is not the case. After presenting an array of perceptions on the topic of anger, Aristotle works through them, finding contrary, overlapping, or analogous notions, concluding that anger contains within it somewhat unruly and disparate elements, too many to allow one to draw definitive hard-and-fast conclusions. But at the same time, the particular cases and the moral sensibilities of the virtuous person, we may find it appropriate for a gentle-minded person to increase one's level of anger where appropriate to hold others accountable for transgressions or defend oneself from unjust attacks, while in another situation, the ruler-type may need to decrease one's level of anger so as to more clearly hear out multiple parties and make a just decision. After all, misdirected anger can lead to the wrongful action, doing much damage to public trust and social stability. And in both cases, the particular elements can only be known in the details of particular agents (with a particular history), in a particular situation, so that one might better know when to express anger, with what person, in what context, in what amount, for how long, and in what manner and so on. All of these elements together make up a way to think and act about anger that in fact highly circumscribes and gives guidance to an agent's understanding and action regarding anger.

The third step of Aristotle's "priority of appearances" method is to—having gathered various phenomena and having given an account of its tensions, contradictions, and redundancies—return to the appearances or phenomena with which we started. The philosopher cannot say anything he or she pleases, but is ultimately accountable to the phenomena at hand, which has directed our gathering of appearances at the beginning of the investigation, and

---

24. Nussbaum, *Fragility of Goodness*, 247.

has brought us full circle now back to itself. And if things do not square off, if the account we have given of the appearances does not align itself with, or ring true to, the phenomena with which we started, then the philosopher has cause to rethink one's project. In our example with Aristotle's exploration on anger, having worked through the multiple phenomena, he returns to the appearance of anger and finds that his project holds up, or at least is not dramatically out of alignment when he says, in effect, the unwieldy nature of this emotion requires that the best we can do is circumscribe it by emphasizing that it must be explored and managed by particular cases.

But this is an area where many go wrong, says Aristotle, in which having gathered the phenomena and having begun processing it, the philosopher takes off on a particular trajectory and stays on it, extending their argumentation to its logical conclusion, without returning full circle to the appearances with which they began. History is filled with examples of abandoned philosophical projects—made manifest by the many "isms" with which we are familiar.

TOLLE AND PLATO'S OFFER OF AN UNTROUBLED LIFE

As Tolle puts it, "When the world is not viewed from the perspective of the formless, it becomes a threatening place, and ultimately a place of despair."[25] What Tolle means by this is that there is an array of elements—injury, ill health, psychological affliction—that can at any moment reverse our fortune. To no fault of our own, such elements can quickly undo our projects, aspirations, indeed our very selves. Try as we may, humans cannot eliminate all risks and misfortune, but we can reduce them, or at least reduce the appearance of them so that we can enjoy a more peaceful life. In this way, as Tolle and Plato have it, the world can look less threatening, when viewed from the perspective of formlessness.

25. Tolle, *New Earth*, 227.

Tolle's Disregard for the Particular

Tolle's and Plato's projects are designed to provide us with some means by which we can reduce affliction and anxiety in our lives. One means by which to do this is by reducing one's bodily appetites, which is important because the appetites of the body, such as food and sexual desire, are unstable by nature. Both desires have the effect of impairing one's judgment, of destabilizing our ability to choose well. Not only do the appetites cause trouble because of the unstable nature of the objects we desire, but they draw upon the less rational elements in our soul (in contrast to the "rational"—for Plato—and the "Presence"—for Tolle—part our souls).

The next step in reducing affliction and anxiety is to go to that place of "formlessness"—that place of pure transcendence where we cannot be hurt by the particularities and externalities that surround us—our desires, aspirations, friendship, love, material attachments, and memories. Their power to harm us can be reduced when they are devalued, relativized, and subordinated to that place of formlessness. From the place of transcendence and formlessness, Tolle and Plato have it, the particularities are viewed as "external," mere objects of no great value in comparison to the great value of an interior self in its pure essence.

This devaluation of the many "externals" of our lives has the effect of putting them all on one plane, or in one single grouping, where they are all revalued and relativized in a way that allows us to choose among them with more equanimity and detachment. This singular grouping is a place where all the particularities of our lives—our beliefs, possessions, friendships, loves, emotions, convictions—are homogenized, end up qualitatively the same, differing only by degrees. Put otherwise, they are all grey in color, varying only in shades, the effect being we can more easily choose among them.

An example of the *de* and *re*valuing are found in Tolle's comments about love:

> Love is not selective, just as the light of the sun is not selective. It does not make one person special. It is not exclusive. Exclusivity is not the love of God but the "love"

of ego. However, the intensity with which true love is felt can vary. There may be one person who reflects your love back to you more clearly and more intensely than others, and if that person feels the same toward you, it can be said that you are in a love relationship with him or her. The bond that connects you with that person is the same bond that connects you to the person sitting on the bus, or with a bird, a tree, a flower. Only the degree of intensity with which it is felt differs.[26]

The difference of one's bond with a car and one's significant other is a matter of degree, that is quantitative, and not qualitative, thereby making one's objects of love interchangeable and replaceable. With this line of reasoning, one could ask Tolle what make of an automobile, or how many, would equal my significant other were they to be taken from me. With such a single metric of valuation, the possibilities become much easier to value and choose.

Another example of putting all externalities on the same plane is like asking someone if they want $1,000, $1,500, or $2,000? Of course this choice is made easy by the fact that the options are of the same genus, as it were, on the same plane. But what if one were confronted with the choice of spending limited resources on badly needed plumbing, as opposed to the demand of a European vacation from an unhappy and demanding spouse. Such options are not on the same plane, are not of the same genus, and for this reason are more troubling to those who must choose. Tolle and Plato create a system homogenizing all human particulars, and then reconstituting them as a singular type so that we might be able to choose from a singular group of apples, rather than apples and oranges. Tolle reflects this devaluation/revaluation process as he writes,

> The many things that happen, the many forms that life takes on, are of an ephemeral nature. They are all fleeting. Things, bodies and egos, events, situations, thoughts, emotions, desires, ambitions, fears, drama... they come, pretend to be all-important, and before you know it they

---

26. Tolle, *Power of Now*, 155.

TOLLE'S DISREGARD FOR THE PARTICULAR

are gone, dissolved into the no-thingness out of which they came. Were they ever real? Were they ever more than a dream, the dream of form?[27]

Not only are particularities impermanent, Tolle says, but, like dreams, it is questionable if they exist at all. They present themselves as important, but in fact come and then dissolve into the "no-thingness" from which they came. On the one hand, our whole lives will appear as a dream as we approach death; on the other hand, he goes on to say, such dreams have a purpose: "to make you aware of the fleetingness of every situation, which is due to the transience of all forms, your attachment to them lessens, and you disidentify from them to some extent."[28]

To sum up, Tolle and Plato hold out the promise of a less-troubled, less-afflicted life that involves three steps: the first is to detach from bodily appetites; the second is to disidentify from particularities—"bodies and egos, events, situations, thoughts, emotions, desires, ambitions, fears, drama"; the third is to devalue and revalue the particularities of one's life by grouping them from the place of formlessness, detachment and transcendence.

ARISTOTLE'S CRITIQUE OF TOLLE AND PLATO'S DEVALUED AND REVALUED LIFE

To begin with, Aristotle would say, this kind of talk is not human talk. Our talk—human talk—is based upon human experience developed over time. Our talk and our good is a species-specific good, which is to say our human talk and our human good is not the talk and good of nonhuman animals or extraterrestrials. The talk and good of, say, grazing animals is another good, another talk. Nor is our good a purely transcendent good, for that would be a good and a talk of angels or gods. We must not speak of our human good as a good in general, in an unqualified way that speaks on behalf of all creatures and gods. As Nussbaum puts it, "If the

---

27. Tolle, *New Earth*, 209.
28. Tolle, *New Earth*, 225.

essential features of lives are not the same across the species, as it looks evident to Aristotle that they are not, then the search for the good life must be a species-relative, rather than a general search. I cannot choose for myself the good life of an ant, a lion, a god."[29] Aristotle would say that Tolle is speaking on behalf of the good life of angels or a god, and that such a good may be the good of a god, but it is not the good of an ant, a lion, or a human. It is a life that is not available to us as mortals, and as such we should not seek it. Were we to seek it, we would do so at the expense of some element of our humanity.

Aristotle will not get into an argument with Tolle and Plato regarding the "unitary, unchanging Being of the universe,"[30] and that they cannot be proved wrong based upon some scientific, foundational evidence. What he says is that such claims about the nature of creation are comical, that such speakers are in no position to say what they say. Speaking of the Eleatic school of philosophy that maintained—as does Tolle and Plato—that matter is corrupted, illusory and therefore serves as a distraction, Nussbaum makes the following Aristotelean argument:

> Just as a person blind from birth is in no position to use in an argument premises about colors, since he can have no experience of color, so the Eleatic is in no position to use in an argument premises having to do with the unitary, unchanging Being of the universe. Change and plurality are in everything we experience.... The Eleatic is "comical" because he does not succeed in singling out or indicating the unchanging, undivided One. This unity is, by the Eleatics own story, "far from the beaten path of human beings." Neither he nor anyone else in his community can have an experience of it. Therefor Aristotle would say he cannot introduce it into discourse; discourse, even when vague and imprecise, is bounded by the experience of the group. Therefore, though the Eleatic believes he is saying something bold and strange,

---

29. Nussbaum, *Fragility of Goodness*, 293.
30. Nussbaum, *Fragility of Goodness*, 255.

he is really saying nothing at all. This is why we can say that his talk is "mere words" without understanding.[31]

And so, even if such a "unitary, unchanging Being of the universe" exists in the form of a Form, we cannot talk about it, and therefore cannot know it in any meaningful way, because our talk is "bounded by the experience of a group." In this way such talk remains speculative, taking us to places that we cannot inhabit, which is why Aristotle's notion of appearances is so important. It is important because it brings us back to what we know, or can know, based upon our experience. And such knowledge based upon experience is further grounded because it is a shared experience of a language-speaking community, and one that is, in the end, to contribute to the good of that language-speaking community which is also a political community.

Aristotle's opposition to Plato's and Tolle's oneness or singular good, and the homogeneity of beliefs, activities, objects, and externals of the world, brings with it an argument for a plurality of experience and objects. He begins his argument for the non-oneness of experience with talk of the "good," in which what he says could apply equally to Tolle's talk of Being. He says that, straight up, we use the word "good" in different ways. One way in which we refer to "the good" is in terms of Plato's Forms, in which there is an unchanging, transcendent, pure good from which objects and particulars in this world derive their goodness. If this is the case, when we pursue the good of, say, an idea, Plato says, we pursue it for the sake of a greater good of the Form. Aristotle says that when we say we have a "good idea," the good we speak of is not the good of the Form goodness. This goodness does not derive its goodness from the Form, but has a value or goodness in and of itself—that is to say, has an intrinsic value. In other words, we are using the word good and goodness in different ways and with different meanings.

Of course in Plato and Tolle's project they would say all these are unified, are expressions of the Form Good—that the good of friendship is related to the good of physical exercise in that both

---

31. Nussbaum, *Fragility of Goodness*, 255–56.

are derived from the singular Form—Good. Aristotle says, this is not the case—such goods as friendship and physical exercise do not derive their status as good from the Form—Good. They are simply goods, and they are good, because we enjoy them as humans. As with many other goods that humans enjoy, such as playing games, telling jokes, watching sports, listening to music, looking at art, swimming in an open body of water, they are related only by the word we use to describe them (human goods) and do not derive their goodness from a singular Form—Good. Aristotle argues for the variety, separateness, and plurality of goods. But if, on the contrary, thought, sight, etc., also belong to the group of intrinsically good things, the same definition of "good" will have to be manifested in all of them, just as, for example, the definition of whiteness is the same in snow and in white paint. But in actual fact the definitions of "good" as manifested in honor, thought, and pleasure are different and distinct. The good, therefore, is not some element common to all these things as derived from one Form.[32]

Just as we cannot say that the whiteness of snow is the same thing as the whiteness of paint (that a Form, Whiteness, in its transcendent purity, informs and expresses itself through both of them) so, Aristotle tells us that we cannot speak of "the good" as Plato describes it, as a form that expresses itself in the many objects of this world. If this were the case, asks Aristotle, how can we speak of "the good" in these different things? After listing multiple ways that we could speak of "the good" in these disparate and multiform objects, he says that assuming there is "some common good which different things possess in common, or that there exists a good absolutely in itself and by itself, it evidently is something which cannot be realized in action or attained by man."[33] Like the Eleatic school of philosophy, such talk is not of the human world, and so we should not allow ourselves to be distracted by such talk. If we are to talk about goods, Aristotle is saying, we should talk about goods in a way that is accessible to humans and human experience.

---

32. Aristotle, *Nicomachean Ethics*, 1096b 20–25.
33. Aristotle, *Nicomachean Ethics*, 1096b 31–34.

PLATO'S THE GOOD AND TOLLE'S BEING

What Aristotle says of Plato's Form, "the Good," can be said of Tolle's Being. It is worth repeating that Plato's argument to support his notion of the Forms brings with it an argument in support of the notion of singularity, a oneness to life as we experience it. However, humans do not intuitively experience a oneness, argues Aristotle. Like Plato, Tolle argues for a notion of Being as a Form (which, again, he describes as formless) that exists behind, prior to, and in the background to the many forms, externalities, or particularities that make up the human world. As Tolle puts it, but it could just as well have been said by Plato, "Being is prior to existence. Existence is form, content, 'what happens.' Existence is the foreground of life; Being is the background, as it were."[34] Like Plato's Form of the Good, Tolle's "Being is not only beyond but also deep within every [particular] form as its innermost invisible and indestructible essence."[35]

As with Plato, Tolle devalues and revalues particularities as a way to bring them into a total system designed to allow humans to contain and manage them, which allows for better choosing. Tolle too speaks of a singularity and oneness in a way that leaves nothing "separate," which is to say, leaves nothing outside of his system. He refers to and regards "the other" in his writing in the same way in which he regards the many thought-forms that create separateness:

> Identification with your mind creates an opaque screen of concepts, labels, images, words, judgements, and definitions that blocks all true relationship. It comes between you and yourself, between you and your fellow man and woman, between you and nature, between you and God. It is the screen of thought that creates the illusion of separateness, the illusion that there is you and a totally separate "other."[36]

---

34. Tolle, *New Earth*, 220.
35. Tolle, *Power of Now*, 13.
36. Tolle, *Power of Now*, 15.

Eckhart Tolle's Hall of Mirrors

It is worth noting that the talk of "otherness" in much of contemporary thought speaks of that which cannot easily, nor should it, be assimilated into one's "words, judgments, and definitions" and thus stands as a marker that resists and exposes our tendency to create a singular, monolithic system.[37] Usually our talk of "otherness" presupposes a plurality to life, and is displayed by that which cannot be assimilated. But Tolle uses it in the opposite way, suggesting that singularity and oneness are the de facto status of things, and if there is some form of "otherness" out there, it is not because that "otherness" actually exists, but it is there as an illusion of one's making so as to prop up one's ego. In other words, the "other" for Tolle is an invention of the false self, created to animate and sustain itself.

By maintaining the "priority of appearances" Aristotle says that plurality is a feature of the natural and human world, that things exist outside of our knowledge and experience; encounters with such "otherness" for Aristotle are occasions for surprise and delight, as they remind us of the inconclusivity, diversity, and open-endedness of the matter and experience that informs the human world. Promoting this Aristotelean point of view, Nussbaum says,

> Look and see how rich and diverse the ultimate values in this world are. Do not fail to investigate each valuable item, cherishing it for its own specific nature and not reducing it to something else. These injunctions lead to a long and open-ended list—for we would not want to rule out beforehand the possibility of some new item that will turn up whose own separate nature is irreducibly distinct from those we have previously recognized.[38]

We see here that Aristotle's priority of the particular, and plurality that comes with it, embraces surprise and the unexpected—embraces "otherness"—in its refusal to reduce it to something else and by seeking to enjoy and explore it for its own sake. Tolle, on

---

37. Emmanuel Levinas, of course is the philosopher of alterity—of the need to recognize and allow otherness to have a claim on us.

38. Nussbaum, *Love's Knowledge*, 82.

Tolle's Disregard for the Particular

the other hand, regards otherness as illusory because of an anterior knowledge that everything is already subsumed into his system of singularity made possible by the forms and known as Being. For Tolle, so we are arguing, there is no otherness; everything that exists is contained within the Oneness he has been promoting all along. Again, if there is otherness, it is a construct of our imagination designed to create an enemy, so as to reinforce one's ego.

In contrast to Tolle and Plato, whose place of detachment views particulars as fleeting, impermanent, and replaceable, Aristotle has it that there is much in life that is non-interchangeable, irreducibly distinct, and non-replaceable. Our child is like no other child and our loss of her is a cause for grieving, in which the highest level of grieving is experienced by us, the parents of this child. We can learn from other families how one might cope with the loss of a child, but our experiences will be different because our child is not that child and our experience is not that of those parents. Grief is appropriate and called for, but what that grief looks like to us will be "right" and "good" even if it is manifested in different ways. But Tolle's system of thought would qualify our grief, for our relationship to this child is that of any other attachment, an externality, an impediment to our access to true Being. Tolle's system would have it that the loss of such a child, if we are spiritually advanced, would be experienced as fleeting, an experience made possible by a notion that this child is simply another drop in the ocean of Being.

Arguing against Plato (and Tolle, I will show later) Nussbaum says, for Aristotle, "the two things that above all make people love and care for something are the thought that it is all their own and the thought that it is the only one they have";[39] because of this, "our most intense feelings of love, fear and grief are likely to be directed at objects and persons who are seen as irreducibly particular in their nature and in their relationship to us."[40] Indeed, it is the radical particularity of a child as *my* child—irreplaceably and unexchangeable as it is—that makes this attachment all the more intense, and without this sense of the non-replaceability,

---

39. Aristotle, *Politics*, 1262b 22–23.
40. Nussbaum, *Love's Knowledge*, 83.

"a great part of the value and motivating force of the love will be undercut."[41] And of course that undercutting, or devaluing, is something Tolle would welcome as a means of protecting a parent from the grief, fear, and pain that comes with the loss of my child.

Along these lines, Tolle writes, "It is likely you won't feel any emotion when you are told that someone's car has been stolen, but when it's your car, you will probably feel upset. It is amazing how much emotion a little mental concept like 'my' can generate."[42] We find here that Tolle agrees with Aristotle in that the more irreplaceable something is, such as a family member or property, the greater our identification with it, and the more we suffer when it is diminished or removed. But of course Tolle's project is one of removing the causes of grief and fear, at least to the extent possible, in the lives of mortals. And so to remove the causes, or at least minimize this grief, fear, and suffering, Tolle says, our emotional relationship to that which is irreplaceably ours—my car and my child—should be one and the same as with anyone's car and anyone's child. In other words, to Tolle's way of thinking, one's car and one's child should be viewed impersonally, replaceably, exchangeably. Tolle and Plato's project of removing the causes of grief and fear is part of a bigger project of creating an invulnerable self, and indeed creating a Republic, in the case of Plato, and a New Earth, in the case of Tolle, based upon such invulnerability. And so if the world takes away a child, or robs us of a farm or business we have spent a lifetime creating, we are to feel there is a ready supply of similarly valuable (or de-valuable) items somewhere ready to replace it. Also, we should have known these things were impermanent and at risk of being lost or robbed from the beginning, and so why the worry over the loss of a mere human relationships, a mere parcel of land, a mere form of livelihood? It's because we over-identified with whatever it was. We indulged in the delusion that these external objects were more than fleeting in the first place.

From Aristotle's point of view, the question that arises, writes Nussbaum, is "whether his [Plato's] single-valued world

---

41. Nussbaum, *Love's Knowledge*, 39.
42. Tolle, *New Earth*, 233–34.

can possibly have the richness and inclusiveness of the current world. A world in which wealth, courage, size, birth, and justice are all put into the same scale and weighed together, made in their nature expressions of a single thing, will turn out to be a world without any of these items, as now understood. And this, in turn, looks likely to be an impoverished world: for we value these items enough in their separateness not to want to trade them all in."[43] And so we can minimize grief, fear, and anxiety by devaluing the particularities of this world, including of course that which is irreplaceable, and then revalue them. But such devaluing and then revaluing brings with it a loss of the richness and inclusivity, and an "impoverishment" of the human world, and of course with that our very humanity.

43. Nussbaum, *Fragility of Goodness*, 296.

4

That's Just a Story

*Tolle, Plato, and Aristotle
and the Use of Narrative*

IN THIS CHAPTER WE will explore how Tolle and Plato share a common dislike for narrative in general, and specifically, in the case of Plato, for Greek Tragedy. Their main criticism is twofold: that story is imitative of the real, and not the real itself; and that it comes from and contributes to an emotional life that becomes the source of instability and delusion. In contrast to this we will look at Aristotle's high regard for narrative, in particular Greek tragedy, the value of the emotions it generates, and the critique this exacts upon Tolle's anti-narrative stance.

Tolle and Plato share a common concern regarding the power of storytelling in shaping human emotions and the effect narrative has upon identity and action. While Tolle is more focused on the psychology of storytelling, in terms of individual identity, Plato is more concerned with the stories told by Greek tragedians, and its negative consequences upon the politics of the Republic.

While Tolle is less concerned with the political/cultural consequences of storytelling, and more concerned with the individual psychological effects, he effectively illustrates how the two overlap. An example he gives is how the experience of being mistreated can generate a "delusional system" of belief in which one's "sense of being a victim, of being wronged by so many people, makes him feel very special. In the story that forms the basis of his delusional system, he often assigns to himself the role of both victim and hero who is going to save the world or defeat the forces of evil."[1] In this way, the culturally available stories of good and evil, with its heroic characters and victims, are appropriated by individuals in our projects of constructing personal stories.

The alarm Tolle sounds against storytelling is that "it is important to recognize here that the story and the thought forms that make up the story, whether people agree with it or not, have absolutely nothing to do with who you are. Even if people agree with it, it is ultimately, a fiction."[2] The suggestion that the narrative elements to human life are by definition fictitious, which is to say, unreal and untrue, is a theme that runs throughout his teaching. Indeed, *fiction* is at times not a strong enough word. When it comes to other people telling you who they are, according to Tolle, one should be on high alert in terms of how others present themselves, for some, "driven by the ego's feeling of insufficiency and its need to be 'more,' lie habitually and compulsively. Most of what they tell you is a complete fantasy, a fictitious edifice the ego has designed for itself to feel bigger, more special. Their grandiose and inflated self-image can sometimes fool others, but usually not for long. It is then quickly recognized by most people as a complete fiction."[3] And so "fiction," "fantasy," "emotional story-making,"[4] "mental movie making,"[5] and "human drama"[6] are all terms employed by Tolle designed to disparage the narrative elements to human life, elements that promote mere opinions and delusion, as opposed to a self-understanding that is based in "facts."

1. Tolle, *New Earth*, 120.
2. Tolle, *New Earth*, 43.
3. Tolle, *New Earth*, 118.
4. Tolle, *New Earth*, 135.
5. Tolle, *Power of Now*, 18.
6. Tolle, *New Earth*, 200.

Eckhart Tolle's Hall of Mirrors

Plato shares Tolle's mistrust of storytelling which, in Plato's time, came in the form of myths and the Greek theater of the tragic poets. Plato's criticism of storytelling in general was that it was imitative and illusory, rather than real. Stories and storytelling may have entertainment value in their re-creation of something in the world, but tell us little of what is real.

We spoke in the last chapter of Plato's Forms which, as he puts it, enjoy a pure, ideal, and transcendent existence remote from human life. Bedness, we discussed, was one of the Forms, one that the joiner based her product upon. We saw in the dialogues Socrates makes the argument that the painting of the bed is an imitation of the joiner's bed, making it, therefore, twice removed from the real, the Form Bedness. In Book X of the *Republic*, Plato shifts the focus of the imitative painter of the bed to that of the imitative dramatists of the Greek theater who are

> imitators of the images of virtue, and of other things about which they compose, but that they do not attain to the truth: but as we just now said, a painter who himself knows nothing about the making of shoes, will draw a shoemaker, who shall appear to be real to those such as are not intelligent, but who view accordingly to the colour and figure.... In the same manner, I think, we shall say that the poet colours over with his names and words certain colours of the several arts, whilst he understands nothing himself, but merely imitates, so as to others such as himself who view things in his compositions, he appears to have knowledge.[7]

In this way, Plato argues, the dramatists imitate what is real in a way that gives the appearance that they know real virtue when in fact they do not. What they do know is how to employ theatrical devices such as meter, music, plot, staging, character, in a way that manipulates the emotions of the audience. In this way, Plato goes on to say, the dramatist "knows nothing worth mentioning

---

7. Plato, *Republic*, 601a–b.

That's Just a Story

in those things which he imitates, but that imitation is a sort of amusement, and not a serious affair."[8]

In the last chapter we talked about Plato's project of empowering humans to minimize personal grief, loss, and affliction through the devaluation and revaluation of human particularities—attachments to particular people, beliefs, emotions and objects that make up actual human living. This devaluation and revaluation involves, as Plato argues, firstly an ascending of one's perspective, and from that place of transcendence, a process of numbering, measuring and weighing[9] the particularities. From that place of detachment one could then go about one's life dealing with difficult choices in a less troubled way through the use of the "rational" part of one's soul. Plato's protest regarding dramatic theater is that it bypasses the rational part of the soul and appeals to the irrational—which includes the emotional—part of the soul.

Plato believed that tragic theater, especially the plays of Homer, had a negative effect upon the audiences, audiences that included the citizens of Athens as well as the citizens of his imagined Republic: "For somehow, the best of us, when we hear Homer, or any of the tragic writers, imitating some of the heros when in grief, pouring forth long speeches in their sorrow, bewailing and beating their breasts, you know we are delighted; and yielding ourselves, we follow along, and sympathizing with them, seriously commend him as an able poet whoever most affects us in this manner."[10] Plato's main criticism of the tragedians of Athens is that such storytelling animates the non-rational part of one's soul, that part of the soul that includes the emotions. This could not be allowed for Plato in his city, for the city's well-regulation depended upon a citizenry directed by the rational part of the soul, not the irrational.

Tolle's notion of ego functions much like Plato's non-rational part of the soul: both are that part of the self or soul that engages with particulars of human life—our bodily existence, the people

---

8. Plato, *Republic*, 602b.
9. Plato, *Republic*, 602e.
10. Plato, *Republic*, 605d.

we know and care about, attachments, the stories we tell, and the emotions that come with it. Likewise, Tolle's "Consciousness" functions much like Plato's rational part of the soul in that the ideal for both is that they are detached so that they might operate from a place of transcendence, objectivity, purity, and emotional detachment.

TOLLE'S "EMOTIONAL STORY-MAKING" AND ARISTOTLE'S "NARRATIVE EMOTIONS"

In terms of the relationship between emotions and thinking, Tolle writes, there is a "vicious circle between unexamined thoughts and emotions, giving rise to emotional thinking and emotional story-making."[11] Such "emotional thinking" is dealt special abuse from Tolle in two ways: firstly that it is "unexamined," which is to say one is unaware of it, that it does not come under the auspices of reason and awareness; secondly because emotional thinking gives way to story-making, and story-making brings with it an implicit act of interpreting. Tolle, like Plato, assumes that, because the self or soul is more enlightened living an unsullied existence apart from one's earthly attachments, one can animate a true self that experiences the real directly, bypassing, as it were, the need for interpretation. Interpretation suggests for Tolle (and Plato) a kind of narrative activity that removes us from the object, or the pure Form of the object. Allowing something like emotions to play such a determinative role in one's thinking, in our scheme of practical wisdom, is deeply problematic for Tolle, as discussed in the second chapter, because emotions are tied to particularities and objects in the world that are inherently unstable and mutable, and therefore should not be determinative in an agent's overall thinking, choices, and actions.

In contrast, Aristotle holds storytelling in high esteem and does so because he believes storytelling plays an important role in how humans learn to be human. This is because he believes that

---

11. Tolle, *New Earth*, 135.

emotions are a necessary part of what makes us human, and that emotions are learned through our experience of stories. The emotions of pity and fear, Aristotle believed, are indispensable for human agency in that they serve to bond us to others in ways that are necessary for human flourishing. However, such emotions cannot be taught in the same way that, for example, a philosophical belief or a mathematical theory can be taught, that is, cannot be taught directly or prescriptively. That this is the case is because emotional intelligence is achieved through one's entering into the structure of stories. Stories make it possible to access forms of life, forms in which the audience members are not just observers who view characters, plot, and action from a detached point of view; rather the audience is more of a participant in the story, which is brought about through one's identification with one character or another. It is there, from within a story, that we are exposed to a form of life—a fully-realized world of character, plot, and action—that instills and nurtures emotions that we otherwise might lack.

There is a logic that comes with different types of story, each with its own emotional landscape. The action-hero film, the romantic comedy, film noir, the Western, each has its own devices, each has a different set of coordinates within which we, the audience, are located, each promoting different sets of feelings. Among the different kinds of stories and the different story tellers, the tragedians of ancient Athens, as Nussbaum puts it, were understood

> to be the central ethical teachers and thinkers of Greece, the people to whom, above all, the city turned, and rightly turned, with its questions about how to live. To attend a tragic drama was not to go to a distraction or a fantasy, in the course of which one suspended one's anxious practical questions. It was, instead, to engage in a communal process of inquiry, reflections, and feeling with respect to important civic and personal ends.[12]

Aristotle agrees with Tolle and Plato that storytelling in the form of the tragedies has an imitative element, but is not an imitation of a transcendent Form, as it was for Plato, nor an emotional

---

12. Nussbaum, *Love's Knowledge*, 15.

form, as it is for Tolle. We may recall how Plato employs a metaphor in which the portrait painter is one who creates forgeries from the original, forgeries that are three times removed from the original; in contrast to this, Aristotle creates a metaphor of the portrait painter who imitates, to be sure, but in whose imitation makes "something more beautiful than the original."[13]

A central theme or assumption in tragedy is that being of good character and living a good life so far does not secure for us enduring happiness and fullness of good living. The literary device within the tragic form of drama has it that, despite being a good person, going about life as responsibly and as decently as one can, unexpected events and misfortune can nevertheless visit us. And this suggests that the human actor is vulnerable to misfortune, despite one's efforts to shore up our ramparts. There is, as it were, a "contingent" element to human life, and such contingency is embedded in the genre of Greek tragedy.

Invariably, there is a turn of events in tragedy theater that affects something or someone the main character cares about, a plot device that forces the audience to ask the question about what it is we care, the proper way of caring about it, and how the loss of which will play out emotionally.

Another element of the Greek tragedy is the primacy of action over character. Tragedies can do with less than robust main (and tragic) characters, but they cannot do with less than robust action. Tragedies require characters of action, characters who act upon the world. Aristotle has much to say about action, including the extent to which one's agency is realized through action. Action is required of humans, for Aristotle, because of our lack of self-sufficiency and dependence upon objects in the world. Action amounts to "reaching out for something in the world, grasping after some object in order to take it to oneself. Both human and non-human animals, in their rational and non-rational actions, have in common that they stretch forward, so to speak, toward pieces of the world which they attain or appropriate."[14] Our human

---

13. Aristotle, *Poetics*, 1454b 10.
14. Nussbaum, *Fragility of Goodness*, 275–76.

movement, our action, toward the world is the result of human vulnerability and lack of self-sufficiency, both physical and psychological. Action is indispensable to the tragic genre because action is invariably what brings about tragedy, sometimes through acting impulsively, sometimes disregarding signs or warnings, and sometimes through the creation of obstacles that impede one's actions.

We have looked at tragedy as a form of storytelling that, firstly, creates a separation between the goodness of a character, on the one hand, and the unintended misfortune brought upon them on the other hand. Secondly, we have looked at the indispensability of action along with character and plot. That is, in tragedy, one can have a less than developed character engaging in specific actions; but a good tragedy cannot have it the other way around—a developed character disengaged from action. A third element in the logistics of a good tragedy involves the setting up of the tragic character so that pity and fear are experienced by the audience.

A few comments on Aristotle and his understanding of emotions are in order. Aristotle believed that there is a "composite" of primary emotions—pain, pleasure, anger, joy, fear, desire, etc.—but that these emotions do not exist independently from the beliefs we have about life. These primary emotions, Aristotle says, attach themselves to one's particular beliefs, and inform them in our day-to-day experience. So, for example, we talked in chapter 3 about Aristotle's notion of anger, and that one's experience of anger comes from the belief that we have been wronged. Surely we experience a basic pain from such an injustice, but we also experience anger—an emotion that seeks to right the injustice. In a sense anger informs one's experience of injustice. And so, as Nussbaum argues, if it can be demonstrated to me that no such injustice happened, that it was the result of a misunderstanding, then the anger would be gone. Or, if the anger is still there, it can be pointed out that it is an inappropriate emotional response to the situation.

In a similar way Aristotle points out that pity is one's experience of pain in the pain and suffering of another. The purpose of tragic theater is to educate its audience in practical wisdom by setting up a plot in which we experience the pain and suffering of those who, through no fault of their own, fall prey to misfortune. In this context, such pain on the part of the audience (not on the part of the tragic character in the play) is more specifically captured in the word *pity*.

Another element that is required for a tragic story to work is that it must be set up in a way that the tragic character cannot be blameworthy for the misfortune visited upon her, that the tragedy cannot be attributed to her bad choices. If it is the case that the audience feels that the misfortune is due to bad choices then, Aristotle believes, we are unable to feel pity. As he puts it, "Let pity be defined as pain in a man caused by what appears to be a destructive or painful evil which befalls another who does not deserve it, and which the man would think that he himself or someone close to him might be the victim of the same evil in the near future."[15] For the tragic story to work, the audience has to be able to see how they themselves are vulnerable to the same misfortune as the character in the play.

There are constraints within which the tragic poet must work to create a tragic character with whom we, the audience, can identify. On the one hand, they cannot be too similar to us, for if they are, we know their flaws and thus have greater trouble sympathizing with them. On the other hand, they cannot be too unlike us, "for great evil which might befall him appears [to him] to have befallen those more than others who differ in age or any other traits."[16] Likewise, another device in tragedy is that the main character is better than us. As Aristotle puts it, "For comedy sets out to imitate men who are worse than average, tragedy men who are better than average."[17] When misfortune visits those who are "better than average," we learn, Aristotle argues, that we are not invulnerable creatures, but are vulnerable to events beyond our control. On the other hand, the tragic character cannot be too

---

15. Aristotle, *Rhetoric*, 1385b.
16. Aristotle, *Rhetoric*, 1382a.
17. Aristotle, *Poetics*, 1448a15–16.

morally superior to us for, if she is, she is once again beyond the range of the audience's sympathy and believability.

Aristotle generates a list of those who are predisposed to pity, which includes "those who think that evil might be before them; and those who have been victims of it; and those who have escaped it; and the elderly, because they think rightly or by experience; and those who tend to be cowardly; and those who are educated, for they are reasonable; and those who, being any of the above, have parents living, or children, or wives, for these are close to them and might be victims of such evil."[18] Such a list seems to be made up of a disparate grouping, but with a common element—that those predisposed to pity have experienced or are aware of human vulnerability. And among the misfortunes that beset characters in tragic theater, Aristotle says, are "death, bodily injury, affliction, old age, disease, lack of food; evils whose cause is chance are, for example, friendlessness, scarcity of friends . . . deformity, weakness, mutilation, evil from an action whose source ought to have ended in something good; and the frequent repetition of above."[19] What characterizes this list are agents who experience calamity through no fault of one's own.

Another narrative emotion that tragic theater generates is fear. Like pity, fear associates itself with beliefs. Just as pity associates with one's witnessing the misfortune of another, fear is the response to the belief that the misfortune of another could happen to us, and that it could happen to us in the near future. Aristotle says fear of death is generally something humans can keep at a distance, due in part to the effects of friendship, possessions, and achievements.

Unlike Tolle and Plato, Aristotle believes that there is much in life that one should rightly fear, that there is that which can undo or diminish the happiness and security of even the most virtuous person, and that central to what tragedy has to teach us is that such misfortune can be visited upon oneself. Because Tolle's and Plato's practical wisdom maintains that the good or enlightened person

18. Aristotle, *Rhetoric*, 1385b24–30.
19. Aristotle, *Rhetoric*, 1386a7–13.

has little to fear, they find themselves unable to identify with tragic characters; such inability translates into an inability to see that misfortune can be visited upon themselves; being insulated from such emotions prevents them from sympathy toward those who experience misfortune, as well as reinforces their belief that they are immune from it.

Previously we looked at Aristotle's list of types of people who are predisposed to emotions of pity and fear generated by the tragic theater. He also lists those who are not predisposed to the emotions of pity and fear. They include "those who have been completely ruined," and "those who think themselves happy beyond all bounds."[20] Those who "have been completely ruined" will not be able to experience pity because they feel that no further misfortune exists for them—that they have seen it all; and those "who think themselves happy beyond all bounds"[21] are incapable of pity because they have in their possession everything there is, including the absence of misfortune.

Plato and Tolle believe that if one governs oneself by the rational part of the soul (in the language of Plato), or if one lives in consciousness (in the language of Tolle), the person's essential self cannot be harmed in any serious way. Thus, in these two systems of thought, pity is a useless and irrational emotion. Those then acting without the emotions of pity and fear all too easily can find the victims of misfortune at fault, and thus respond to their plight dismissively. Plato did this with Socrates. As Nussbaum describes it,

> In the *Phaedo*, which is a clear case of Platonic antitragedy, there is repeated stress on the fact that Socrates' predicament is not an occasion for pity (cf. Int. I). The bad things are trivial, because they are happening only to his body; his soul is secure and self-sufficient. Accordingly, the dialogue's end replaces tragic pity with a praise of a good man's goodness. In *Republic* X, pity is again singled out for special abuse in connection with the attack upon tragedy. Tragic poetry, Socrates says, does

---

20. Aristotle, *Rhetoric*, 1385b20–21.
21. Aristotle, *Rhetoric*, 1385b20–21.

That's Just a Story

harm to practical rationality, in that "after feeding fat the emotion of pity there, it is not easy to restrain it in our own experiences."[22]

Plato and Tolle both promote a notion of wisdom that tells us the virtuous person (in the case of Plato), and the conscious person (in the case of Tolle) have little to fear, for the things that really matter cannot be damaged or destroyed. As Nussbaum puts it, "Plato's argument, repeatedly, is that correct beliefs about what is and what is not important in human life remove our reasons for fear. The good person attaches no importance to any external loss, to any loss, that is, in a sphere of life that is beyond the control of the rational soul."[23]

Tolle too tells us we have little to fear once we rid ourselves of attachments, which is to say, end our identification with forms: "The underlying emotion that governs all the activity of the ego is fear. The fear of being nobody, the fear of nonexistence, the fear of death. All its activities are ultimately designed to eliminate this fear, but the most the ego can do is cover it up temporarily with an intimate relationship, a new possession, or winning at this or that.... Why fear? Because the ego arises out of identification with form, and deep down it knows that no form is permanent, that they are all fleeting."[24]

Indeed, it is the central thesis of this book that Tolle is every bit the anti-tragedian writer as Plato. Just as Plato bans the tragic poets from the Republic, Tolle bans storytelling from his New Earth. In this way there is a dramatic connection between Tolle's abuse heaped upon narrative, his overall anti "emotional story-making" stance, and his long list of the self-created ways in which agents suffer. At the core of Tolle's project is that those who are victims of misfortune, in the Greek tragedian sense that Aristotle is interested in, are not in fact victims of circumstances and chance, but are creators of, or at least are collaborators in, their own suffering. It is no coincidence that in all of Tolle's writings, which in

---

22. Nussbaum, *Fragility of Goodness*, 385.
23. Nussbaum, *Fragility of Goodness*, 386.
24. Tolle, *New Earth*, 80.

great part deal with human suffering, one is hard pressed to find examples of suffering in which Tolle describes as resulting from no fault of one's own. It is this book's argument that Tolle's system of thought, or more specifically those who subscribe to it, should be added to Aristotle's list of those who are unable to identify with tragic characters in Greek tragic theater and therefore fail in the appropriation of the narrative emotions of pity and fear.

The task here is not to argue what the causes of human suffering might be; rather our task is to make clear the thesis that Tolle's anti-story and tragedian position instills in its followers an attitude of indifference to those who suffer due to their human attachments, their identification with human thought, emotion, and social forms. A good example of this is Tolle's YouTube video entitled "What Can We Learn through Betrayal?" in which he begins by reading a letter from a follower who, after confessing that she feels betrayed, asks,

> "What is to be learned from being betrayed?" Now, of course, *betray* is already a word that is quite heavy, [pause] "He betrayed me" [speaking very slowly], "She betrayed me," there's already a huge amount of heaviness and story in that. If you put it slightly differently it could sound like this: He is a human being and he manifested behavior that corresponded to his level of consciousness at that particular time when he did it. Perhaps at other times, when I met him, he seemed to be at a higher level of consciousness, but then he fell back to a more unconscious state and then his behavior manifested that. Where's the betrayal? It suddenly disappeared. So, that makes it easier on you to deal with it and then to impose a huge narrative of judgment on another person and involve you in this dreadful act in which you become a part, the act of betrayal. Yes, of course you suffered; we all suffer; we all encounter humans who make us suffer, because many humans, most of them, are unconscious and they're not always at the same level. It's an interesting fact that humans can be at enormously varying levels of consciousness, according to the situations they find themselves in. There are conditions in which

humans have the potential for committing a crime, but circumstances never put them in the position where their potential becomes actualized and it can happen that other humans encounter a situation that is very challenging and brings out all the worst accumulations within them that come up to the surface and suddenly turn into these monsters and before you might have known a completely different person, a completely different level of consciousness. So humans get challenged or encounter situations that bring out certain aspects of their unconsciousness between, in sexual encounters, the betrayal has something to do with a man going off with another woman. Not unlikely. That is an area where that kind of attraction that can make people very quickly very unconscious. There are expressions for that. I won't say what. So, yes, the unfortunate thing with human beings—they're not fully enlightened. So, and then you say "I trusted him. He promised me when we got married that he would be faithful, and I trusted him." I'm sure when he promised it he meant it. I don't think that, when he promised to be faithful, he meant "I'm not really going to do that." When he promised to be faithful he meant it. But then a few years passed and, one day, he had a few drinks he looked at that woman there and he was gone [audience laughs], completely unconscious.[25] And again, in Jesus words, forgive them, for they know not what they do. Now to forgive them, is only something you do for yourself because you free yourself of the burden of

---

25. Of course this begs the question, how do we know that the betrayal was the unconscious act? Why could we not say that he sees himself having lived his whole life in delusion, unconsciously attached to the social form of marriage, inhabiting a role called "the husband." Why would Tolle not say that his act of betrayal was actually his true self finally realized that was at work? Tolle's (theoretical) answer to this might be that the betrayal was an exception to an otherwise predictable and consistent life, and that the betrayal is out of character for him. But "character" is Aristotle's idea of what makes for a "true self," something that is constituted by the many forms, roles, and habits, beliefs, intentions, history that Tolle has been dismissing as *ego*. The bottom line is that Tolle's assumption that the husband's act of betrayal was the moment of unconsciousness brings him, Tolle, face to face with a dilemma in terms of how to tell this story, and with it brings a problem for his schema.

having to live with the narrative or a story of betrayal, and be part of that and then part of your sense of identity—this is very painful, but seductive—part of our ego-identity is "I am the one who has been betrayed." And it's a dreadful burden to carry in your sense of self. So if you believe in that story that your mind has created—the act of betrayal, he betrayed me—so you're setting up for yourself an enormous amount of suffering, because that story will become part of your sense of self. And, if that's the case, then it will influence and color from now on the way which you relate to other men or women, whatever it is, can easily color that so, you have to be very careful what you are doing to yourself by creating these stories. They, on a conventional level, they are true. You can say he betrayed me, by the conventional use of language. But it's not the real truth. You might have heard of Byron Katie, the spiritual teacher; she always questions whatever thoughts the mind produces, and that's a wonderful thing because otherwise you might feel tempted to believe in every thought that comes into your head—he betrayed me! And of course Byron Katie would ask "Do you know that for sure? How do you know that." "Yes, of course I know. . . ." And then eventually, if it works, the person can then disidentify with the thought that the mind has created and become free of being trapped by this thought, which means conscious is trapped by this thought that the mind has created. And you are trapped in it. So, be careful with the stories that the mind creates and sometimes if you rephrase, as I just did for you, rephrase the story it suddenly does not cling to you anymore and it no longer becomes part of your identity, your painful identity, your sense of self; you want to be free of that.[26]

Many elements of Tolle's project come together in this talk in which he sets out to answer the woman's question, "What is to be learned from being betrayed?" By Aristotle's definition of literary tragedy, her story meets the conditions of a tragic character: that misfortune was visited upon her to no fault of her own, and that

26. Tolle, "What Can We Learn through Betrayal?"

there was nothing she could have done to prevent it. According to Aristotle's theory, Tolle and his audience should have responded to her account with pity and fear, pity in the sense that they can identify with her and fear in that this is something that could happen to them. But this is not the case. Tolle and his audience demonstrate neither emotion, instead appearing to be dismissive. Why is this the case?

Tolle may be correct in his argument that her "he-did-this-to-me" account is overstated, that is, her former partner's transgression was not directed (so we can assume) toward his wife, but rather the damage to her was collateral. His intention was not to hurt her, but rather to pursue his desire for another woman. Tolle counsels her by replacing a first-person, storied account of "he betrayed me," with an impersonal, third-person account in which "he is a human being and he manifested behavior that corresponded to his level of consciousness at that particular time when he did it. Perhaps at other times, when I met him, he seemed to be at a higher level of consciousness, but then he fell back to a more unconscious state and then his behavior manifested that."

As discussed in chapter 1, central to Tolle's (and Plato's) project is to free us from suffering, which he does by directing the experience from "myself" to "nobody" in particular, from the particular to the universal, from the personal to the impersonal, from story to a neutral reporting. By removing her from a first-person account, his intention is to reduce the pain of the event. By describing the event in terms of "I am the one who has been betrayed," you are, Tolle says, "setting yourself up for an enormous amount of suffering, because that story will become a part of your sense of self." To limit her suffering, Tolle counsels her to frame the matter as something that did not happen to her, but that this is a "story that your mind has created." Through such a retelling, Tolle distances her from her experience in a way that diminishes her ability to state what happened to her. In so doing, he deprives her of a critical human element—the ability to employ the wits, resourcefulness, and determination that allows us to move forward.

In other words, her ability to say "this happened to me," we are arguing, is what is needed for her to move forward.

Another way of making this point is in terms of her husband. What if he described his transgression in third-person, omniscient terms, rather than in the first person? What difference does it make to me, the reader, as it were, in terms of in a truth and reconciliation meeting between the two, in which he recounts the event in terms of "human beings manifest behavior that corresponded to one's level of consciousness at those times when one does something. When this happens, apologies are due"? In contrast to a first-person account, were he to say, "I was unfaithful to you and I am sorry for that." Obviously, in terms of truth and reconciliation and the ability to move forward, the third-person apology would be unsatisfying, if not hard to see as an apology at all.

Tolle advises her to forgive him, which is "only something you do for yourself because you free yourself of the burden of having to live with the narrative or a story of betrayal, and be part of that and then part of your sense of identity—this is very painful, but seductive—part of our ego-identity is 'I am the one who has been betrayed.'" Here Tolle is counseling her to forgive him for therapeutic reasons—that she might let go of anger so that she might go forward—and not for a reconciliation between the two.[27] Moreover, it is unclear as to how one forgives another without telling a story, in other words, returning to the past, and then arriving at a point in which one can say, "I forgive him." And lastly, there seems an element of the drama here, something that Tolle invariably singles out for abuse—her saying, as it were, something to the effect of "despite all he has done to me, I forgive him."

In contrast to Tolle's "anger therapy," Nussbaum argues that the issue is a matter of what she calls restoring the self: "We must remember that they have not tested the relative helpfulness of anger therapy by contrast to other devices for restoring the self, such as work, friendship, shopping, exercise. Therapy invites the betrayed person to focus hours and hours of mental and emotional

---

27. This is a bit out of character for Tolle, as he will occasionally disparage the therapeutic profession.

energy on the person who has left, when, as I have suggested, what she really needs to do is to learn how to go forward—to enjoy. Being alone, to cultivate a range of friendship and activities."[28]

Two things are worth noting regarding Nussbaum's advice to the betrayed character. The first is that her counsel of "restoring the self" is one of cultivating new particularities in one's life, of finding new attachments, so to speak, and not a matter of transcending the story of betrayal. Secondly, Nussbaum's advice is about envisioning new possibilities, which is to say, imagining a new future.[29] Lastly, it is advice about action—the act of finding new friends, engaging in exercise, and finding new activities—all of which are not deeply interior things, but are externalities, which is to say are forms that Tolle disparages. Whereas Tolle tells us that doing must come out of Being, Nussbaum is telling us that there are times when we must retrain ourselves by simply doing, in which case Being comes out of doing.

At this point, Tolle and the tragic character have described matters in terms of betrayal. We have suggested that her task is not so much to transcend, but to restore the self, and to do this one must imagine and create, through action, a new future. But this is easier said than done when we considered the effects of a lifetime of intermingling with another. With separation comes the experience of abandonment, of being on one's own, and grief of what has been lost. Betrayal is a complicated word, one that describes a composite of emotions: pain, grief, abandonment, and anger. Tolle's point is that we set ourselves up for suffering when

28. Nussbaum, *Anger and Forgiveness*, 126.

29. Regarding this, it is very hard to imagine what Tolle's continued advice of "the power of now," in terms of what its emphasis on living in the present moment, has to offer us. Indeed, in terms of any crisis in one's life, we typically look back to examine our successes and failures, what we do well and not so well, and with whom, so as to decide where to go from here. Thus the notion of narrative, the notion of telling our own story, is always a matter of firstly looking back, as we can only know (and revise) our story retrospectively. Few of us think of us in our day-to-day lives in narrative terms, as that would involve a good deal of self-drama. Rather, it is at moments of crisis, when change is required, that we take stock, as it were, of our lives in a narrative manner, to allow us to redirect.

we identify with forms; to love another is to entangle oneself with something that is unstable, impermanent, and uncertain. Thus Tolle's corrective is to transcend to Being, to become detached from particulars, to remind ourselves that life is fleeting. Tolle's counsel is, if we find ourselves troubled and afflicted by human relationships, we have more spiritual work to do.

WAYS WE CAN BE HARMED BY PERSONAL LOSS

Tolle and Plato's project, as we have argued, is one of creating distance between an interior "I" and the external events and personal loss that cause us to suffer. For Tolle, there is no loss or harm so great that more detachment and dis-identification can't take care of. Aristotle is sympathetic to this project in so far as it seeks to increase self-sufficiency and minimize personal grief, but he would argue that the detachment and dis-identification Tolle prescribes comes at too high a price—that price being the human form of life itself. On the one hand, Aristotle argues that we must remain human and work within that form; on the other, we must be honest about the ways in which we can be diminished by the effects of such loss and, in this case, betrayal.

One way a human can be diminished is in being prevented to act. As we said earlier, for Aristotle, action is an intrinsic element to human life. To be human is to act upon the world, and one form of action is social interaction with friends. Aristotle does not separate romantic relationships from friendships in general in that both forms of friendship involve the intermingling of lives. Such intermingling has many elements to it, such as desire for the good of the other, exclusivity, delight in common objects, and shared activities. Aristotle sees these all as forms of action, and when a friendship is ended by one friend abandoning another, the abandoned partner experiences a loss of activity, or an impediment to the activity once enjoyed. Such impeding, Aristotle argues, diminishes one's condition for happiness.

Aristotle makes the case for action as being essential to human agency by arguing that it makes no sense to think of someone as possessing good character, and at the same time being completely inactive. We cannot know what this person is without witnessing their action. He illustrates this by describing a person who, in their youth displayed good character, but in their adult life falls into a coma. As Nussbaum puts it, "Aristotle objects [in both the *Nicomachean Ethics* and the *Eudaimonia Ethics*] that this just is not in harmony with our practices and beliefs. We simply do not think that a state or condition that never does anything is sufficient for living well. It seems incomplete, frustrated, cut off from its fulfillment."[30]

Later Aristotle compares the adult of no action to an athlete that does not compete. A person of good character is similar to an athlete in good condition in that both involve training and preparation that finds its fulfillment in action—virtuous activity for the person of good character and athletic competition for the athlete. Depriving the virtuous character of a place to act virtuously and depriving the athlete of a place to compete diminishes their condition for happiness. And such is the same for the activity of friendship. The removal of a friend is the removal of a place of action that, now gone, diminishes the conditions for happiness for the woman who was betrayed. In this way, impediments to action diminish one's conditions for happiness. In other words, for Aristotle, the loss of interpersonal relationships has the potential to cause lasting harm.

A second way in which tragic harm can diminish the conditions of happiness is circumstances, by which he means misfortunes for which we have difficulty finding something or someone to blame. Similar to the betrayed spouse, Aristotle's list of circumstances that impede our actions are conditions brought about to no fault of one's own: poverty, low social status, physical deformity, ugliness, low intelligence, childlessness—or worse, badly behaved children—and chronic illness, to name a few.

Though such impediments to action due to circumstances are challenging, the person of good character need not be undone: as Nussbaum puts it, for Aristotle, "the stability of character will stand

---

30. Nussbaum, *Fragility of Goodness*, 323.

between him and really bad action. But only bad action makes a person truly *athlios* [wretched], if actions are the main thing in life."[31] And so, on the one hand, good character is not enough to prevent affliction caused by misfortune (indeed, we need action, and the less impeded action the better); on the other hand, good character cannot be done without.

We have discussed how the conditions for happiness of a person of good character (Plato) or a conscious person (Tolle) cannot be harmed by externalities, in Tolle and Plato's scheme of things, and two ways in which this is not the case, in terms of Aristotle. Two ways in which the conditions for happiness for those of good character or conscious persons can be diminished, according to Aristotle, is by that which impedes action and by circumstances of misfortune. It could be said that these two ways of diminishing the happiness of a person come from without.

Aristotle's third way of harming the conditions for happiness has to do with trust. To highlight some themes of trust, Aristotle comments about the differences in character between the young and the old. He speaks at length of what Nussbaum describes as the "virtues of character that the elderly are frequently no longer capable"[32] because the young have not experienced the reversals of fortune that happen over a lifetime. Of the young he has many praiseworthy things to say—that they are capable of high hopes, that they are open and guileless, they are capable of greatness of soul, that they lack excessive concern for money because they have little experience of need,[33] they form friendships easily because they take pleasure in the company of others and do not calculate everything with an eye to advantage.[34]

But underwriting all these and all the virtues is that they are capable of trust that is made possible because they have not yet been deceived.[35] Trust is required of the beloved person or

---

31. Nussbaum, *Fragility of Goodness*, 334.
32. Nussbaum, *The Fragility of Goodness*, 337.
33. Aristotle, *Rhetoric*, 1389a14–15.
34. Aristotle, *Rhetoric*, 1389a35–b2.
35. Aristotle, *Rhetoric*, 1389a18–19.

friend because it allows us to devote our energies of generosity and well-wishing of the other rather than suspicion that the other might diminish us. Trust allows us to enter into common projects with confidence that they will enliven us in the long run rather than become the source of our undoing. The trusting person is more generous because they think less about immediate benefits, and enjoy a confidence that their giving contributes to a larger good from which they, along with others, will benefit.

And of course the trusting person's lack of suspicion makes them more vulnerable to betrayal. Betrayal has perhaps the most deleterious effect upon one's condition for happiness because it is the willful taking of something that is good—trust—and turning it against the trusting person. Examples of trust being used against one are many, and among the most egregious is perhaps the example of sexual abuse. Sexual abuse is often a case in which a trusted member of an institution, community, or household uses that trust to disarm a victim. Few things are more insidious than the spectacle of a good person whose trust has been betrayed, or social spaces where trust is no longer available.

Whereas, the betrayal of trust for Aristotle is perhaps the most serious threat to the conditions for happiness of a human person, Tolle's response to the betrayal experienced by his tragic character is little more than dismissive. That "we all suffer," as he says, is part of the way he dismisses her, but at the core of such dismissiveness is a worldview that undervalues social cohesion, and the trust that makes that cohesion possible. That is, his tone of dismissiveness is due to the belief that humans should not put their trust in other humans (or institutions) in the first place, for such objects are externalities, and therefore are inherently unstable in the first place. Indeed, trust itself is a category that plays little part in Tolle's scheme of things.

5

Angelic Life, Foundations, and Transcendence

MOST OF TOLLE'S TALK of transcendence is about rising above the attachments, particularities, and externalities of human life so as to lessen human affliction so that we might experience the transcendence and timelessness of Being. The criticism I wish to level here is that Tolle fails to examine the various implications that transcendence and immortality carry with them. Like Plato, he simply takes for granted that the human desire to live a long and healthy life means that living a long life is good, living a longer life is better, and living forever is best. As Plato says, it is through sexual desire and generation of offspring that humans and animals display the ultimacy of our desire for immortality.[1] Like Plato, Tolle takes it for granted that immortality is a good thing, and that physical limits should and can be overcome by spiritual means.

Tolle and Plato assume there is a continuity from the human mortal life of limitation to the godlike immortal life without limits. But this is not the case, Aristotle would say. Mortality and immortality are not a continuum in which immortality supersedes mortality; rather it is better to think of them as altogether different realms, each with its own parameters and limitations. To put them

---

1. Plato, *Symposium*, 207d.

Angelic Life, Foundations, and Transcendence

on the same scale is like having a human in an athletic contest compete with another species—say a human swim-racing a dolphin, or a human wrestling a gorilla. Such comparisons and such competitions makes no sense.[2]

In chapter 3, we made the argument that our talk and our good is a species-specific good, which is to say our human talk and our human good is not the talk and good of nonhuman animals or extraterrestrials. This criticism of Tolle has it that he overlooks the following: that talk of transcendence is one in which he confuses two different species, the angelic and the human, or at least he assumes a too-easy continuity between the two. Tolle's program, so we are arguing, is directed to the good of another species, particularly the species of angels, and is not a life that is available to us as mortals, nor should it be. To seek it is at the loss of, or at the expense of, indispensable elements of our humanity.

In this chapter we will look at the downside, as it were, of the transcendence and immortality proposed by Tolle, and why any right-thinking mortal should not desire it. Along with this, we will propose an alternative understanding of transcendence by exploring a story of a particular angel—transcendent and immortal being that he is—who descends, as it were, from the angelic world to our human world. Such a story takes the form of the 1987 movie *Wings of Desire*, directed by Wim Wenders and written by Wim Wenders and Peter Handke.

Wings of Desire was filmed in Berlin, Germany, before the collapse of the wall dividing Communist East Germany from liberal-democratic West Germany. Its premise is simple: the city of Berlin enjoys the presence of angels who mill about, watching human goings-on, unable to be seen by the humans, except for some children and us, the viewers of the movie. The story focuses on one angel in particular, Damiel, who decides to become a human, knowing that doing so means giving up the immortal status he enjoys as an angel.

---

2. This is a central assumption that underwrites Nussbaum's arguments regarding transcendence in her chapter "Transcending Humanity," at the end of *Love's Knowledge*.

Eckhart Tolle's Hall of Mirrors

Damiel, like the other angels in Berlin, is a bit of a voyeur, observing the comings and goings of humans, in which their neediness and vulnerability is on full display. Damiel and his companion angel, Cassiel, go about the city, unable to have any actual affect upon human activity, and yet are sympathetic to the day-to-day human struggles of the residents of Berlin. Angels can be transposed in an instant, one moment in the back seat of a car consoling a pregnant woman, another moment in the public library listening to the inner monologue of an aged storyteller for whom there are no listeners (except the angel). Much of the viewing pleasure of this film is that we see the world as the angels see it—omnisciently—albeit within the technical limits of film as a medium to give us such a sense, and within the limits of how angels perceive. For example, there are many particulars that angels cannot see, such as color. They only see essences which, in terms of color, end up being shades of black and white.

Wenders is attentive to what makes angels what they are and how to depict them in the film. For example, he takes the immateriality of angels seriously by thinking through the implications of such immateriality. As he says, "Even though the angels have been watching and listening to people for such a long time, there are still many things they don't understand. For example, they don't know and can't imagine what colours are, nor can they taste or smell. They can guess what feelings are, but they can't experience them directly. As our angels are basically loving and good, they can't imagine things like fear, jealousy, envy, or hatred. They are familiar with their expression, but not with the things themselves."[3]

Throughout the movie, Damiel shows this lack of understanding of human ways, but in his case, unlike the other angels, it makes him all the more fascinated with mortal life. So, for example, he shares with his friend, Cassiel, detailed observations of human life from his notebook. He gives hints all the while of a desire to relinquish his immortality as an angel in exchange for the human world of risk, vulnerability, and death, but does not take immediate action until a chance encounter with a traveling

3. Wenders, *Logic of Images*, 90.

circus trapeze artist, Marion, whom he observes rehearsing for an upcoming show. Damiel is taken in by her physicality, beauty, and grace on the trapeze.

Another reason Damiel wants to become human is because he wants to have a story which, as an angel, he is unable to have for several reasons. Immortality prevents angels from having a story because stories, by definition, require an ending, and since angelic existence does not have an ending, angels cannot have a story. A great quality of humans is that they are storied creatures because they live in time (not eternity), which is to say we have an end. And it is their collective stories that promote and teach about a most important skill—resourcefulness. It is not a coincidence that Homer's *Odyssey* is a story about a character who rejects the offer of immortality from the goddess, Calypso, and, by his wits and resourcefulness, engineers a safe return by sea to his home and wife on the island of Ithaca. Had Odysseus accepted Calypso's offer of immortality, there would be no story to tell.

Not only do angels not have stories, but their ability to act upon the world is very limited. Their ability to see and deal only in essences, and not in substances or matter, means they have little material effect upon the world. Wenders attempts to illustrate this inability through scenes in which Damiel, while still an angel, picks up such material objects as a stone in one scene, and a pencil in another; in each case, the material object remains unmoved, but the angel takes possession of the object's essence. Also, there is the scene in which Cassiel, despite his best efforts, is unable to prevent a suicide.

Angels operate in universals, essences, or, as Wenders puts it, "in pure CONSCIOUSNESS."[4] But writers of stories, in particular novels or fiction (rather than, say, myths), must attend to particularities for it to be a good story. Operating only in generalities, angels are unable to select particularities, forced to give equal weight to every event, element, object before them. As Wenders says, a good story can never be a simple laying out of "facts." A life, and the events that make up a life, must be interpreted for it to have

---

4. Wenders, *Logic of Images*, 81.

meaning. The average angel is handicapped by its inability to select particular features from a collection of facts, and in this way, is unable to write a story.[5]

Another reason Damiel wants to become human is because he wants to create. Angels live outside of time, are eternal, and so they have no desire to create. However, mortals possess a creative spirit that arises from a desire to extend their mortal lives by leaving something for others beyond their death. We seek to memorialize, so to speak. One could say this is a form of transcendence, and one could argue that, while we know such transcendence can extend our presence in the world, it will not make us immortal. On the one hand, we can say that angels enjoy an existence without limits. But we can also say that with their unlimitedness comes certain limits, such as the inability to create or have a story. Human finitude and our mortality are limits of course, but limits that make many things possible for us that are not possible for angels.

A theme running throughout this book is that humans are subject to chance, misfortune, and calamity, not unlike other animal species. To compensate for this, humans have developed skills and strategies that lessen our vulnerability and increase our sufficiency. Politics, for Aristotle, is one method by which humans lessen vulnerability. And a big part of politics is recognizing and pursuing our common goods, a pursuit that requires individual skills such as courage, temperance, wisdom, and justice. Neither Tolle's transcendent agent nor the angels of Berlin possess or promote these skills because they do not need them in their immaterial worlds.

They do not need to be courageous because they have nothing to protect and defend; angels have no skin in the game, as it were. They have nothing to lose because they are pure spirit, and spirit cannot be diminished, stolen, wounded, or killed. They do not need temperance because they have no bodily appetites to moderate, nor are they vulnerable to the array of addictions that beset humans. Angels need not practice justice, in either its juridical nor distributive forms, because there are no goods to redistribute and

5. Wenders, *Logic of Images*, 81.

Angelic Life, Foundations, and Transcendence

no contracts needed because there is no exchange of goods and services based upon metrics of equal value. Being without lack, angels are inherently without desire, other than the desire put in them by God. But that desire is difficult for mortals to understand because angels are fully satisfied in their immateriality and are invulnerable to the vicissitudes of bodily life. Seeing only essences, Angels do not have imagination[6] because imagination involves imaging particular objects; being eternal, angels cannot imagine alternative future goals because such a future exists in time. Angels cannot experience envy because there is nothing to desire, let alone desire what other angels desire, as they seem indifferent to other angels. Angels appear unsusceptible to anger because they do not suffer the injustice of slights from other angels. Angels were created with the fullness of knowledge; they know everything all at the same time, which is to say, as Tolle would put it, they enjoy a consciousness that appears different than how humans operate. Humans, on the other hand, must learn, says Aquinas, "discursively,"[7] which is to say, must build upon what they have been previously taught.

Angels are without egos and, presumably, without false selves, because they operate in an environment of limitless resources, without scarcity, and without impediments. Humans, on the other hand, live in a world of finite resources, where we must appropriate the goods of creation to sustain and maintain us in places of scarcity, where there are limits, where there is the cold of winter and the heat of summer. In addition to this, humans must endure the threat of crop failures, earthquakes, floods, hurricanes, and epidemics that frustrate and impede the human project of appropriating the goods of the earth for our survival. The natural environment in which we operate sometimes requires risks, and in our risky projects there is success and failure. The absence of these impediments makes Tolle's non-egoic prescription possible for angels in the angel world, but this prescription does not apply, so we are arguing, to humans living in the human world.

---

6. Aquinas, *Summa Theologia*, q. 57.
7. Aquinas, *Summa Theologia*, q. 58.

Eckhart Tolle's Hall of Mirrors

It is worth noting the extent to which Tolle equates ego, and the false self that comes from it, with personal "drama." In Tolle's scheme of things, "Most people are in love with their particular life drama. Their story is their identity. The ego runs their life. They have their whole sense of self invested in it. Even their—usually unsuccessful—search for an answer, a solution, or for healing becomes part of it. What they fear and resist most is the end of their drama. As long as they are their mind, what they fear and resist most is their own awakening."[8] But the movie finds this critique of ego and drama wanting; it is this world without ego, without drama, and without emotion that Damiel seeks to escape, even at the cost of immortality.

Most of Tolle's references to "ego" are in the context of human resistance, that ego-enhancement takes place when a human experiences some kind of opposition or resistance. Tolle's description of resistance as "drama" overlooks the extent to which obstacles in one's life may have a narrative quality. To recognize this does not mean that one necessarily indulges the emotions (the virtue of temperance or moderation may be helpful here), but neither does it mean that such emotional elements should be overlooked. Indeed, such is the case with a track athlete who seeks to overcome wind resistance and gravity through increased training and conditioning.

On the one hand, we mortals must pick our battles in terms of what limitations we seek to overcome and that which we should resist. On the other hand, it is easy to overlook the many forms resistance and limits take in the life of mortals, for whom the maintenance of physical bodies is a constant. The creation and maintenance of shelter for security and maintaining body temperature, acquisition of clothing, shelter, clean water, food, elimination of waste, not to mention the care for vulnerable others whose limits would overwhelm them were it not for outside assistance, are all forms of resistance. It is little wonder that many of our stories are stories of overcoming limits. To describe efforts to manage limits as "ego-intensification," as Tolle does, is to underestimate the

---

8. Tolle, *Power of Now*, 182.

Angelic Life, Foundations, and Transcendence

vulnerability of the body and bodily existence. Indeed, it is to promote an angelic life, a life that is not bodily, one that therefore does not experience the limits and obstacles that mortals experience.

There are other ways in which Tolle's talk of the ego belongs to the angel world, and not the human. As he says, "Another aspect of the emotional pain that is an intrinsic part of the egoic mind is a deep-seated sense of lack or incompleteness, of not being whole."[9] Angels experience completeness, but can do so because they are pure spirit and thus lack in nothing. Without bodies, they have no appetites and desires. As we have said, a major message of Greek tragic theater is that bodily existence is precarious; mortals can suffer misfortune at any time and to no fault of our own. Thus, human solidarity is informed by the recognition that we are not self-sufficient, that we are incomplete, and therefore depend upon others as they depend upon us. Indeed, it could be said the "social fabric" is held together by the emotions of pity and fear—pity for the misfortune that visits another, and fear that it may happen to us. Again, to describe feelings of incompleteness and fear as "egoic" and something that contributes to a "false self" is deeply problematic, for such emotions motivate us to act upon the world, as well as direct us to the stories, politics, and skills that allow us to survive and hopefully flourish.

Storytelling, imagination, and resourcefulness are some of the qualities that make mortals the very unique (but not unlike other) species we are. Little wonder that when angels fall in love, to the extent that they can fall in love, they do so with humans. In *Wings of Desire*, Damiel's falling in love is a falling in love with a human who cannot be seen as separable from her multiple human qualities: the grace and excellence of the human physical form, such as trapeze grace and strength, story-making, emotional intelligence, the life of the senses, and the skills needed to thrive. Damiel's descending to the human form invites the question as to why mortals would want to transcend to the angel world that Tolle promotes?

---

9. Tolle, *Power of Now*, 45.

Two possible answers come to mind: one is that some people experience this human life as one of suffering to the extent that they desire to be freed from it; the other answer is that some people find human existence so to their liking that they seek to extend it through forms that give a sense of immortality.

As for the first group, few of us need to be compelled to see this. As Aristotle points out, misfortune and the suffering that comes from it can indeed diminish the conditions for happiness, no matter how hard we try to prevent it. This is because extending ourselves, the act of attaching, is in great part what makes us human, and that such attachments create the conditions for stability and resilience, as well as instability and harm. To this, we can only say this is human existence—a temporal existence that is vulnerable and uncertain. A world that is timeless in which we are immortal and invulnerable is not accessible to us. But even if it were accessible, we should not seek it, or at least not seek it without firstly engaging the practical wisdom, resourcefulness, and skills that mortals have relied upon since our beginning.

The second group is mistaken in the way Plato was mistaken when he argued to live long is good; to live longer is better; to live forever is best. It is mistaken because the life-forever world, the immortal world, cannot be viewed as an extension of the human world but, as I have tried to argue, is an altogether different kind of world. To seek it is to change the rules of the game in a way that is not possible.

TOLLE'S HIDDEN HARMONY AND ARISTOTLE'S PRINCIPLE OF NONCONTRADICTION

Many assertions and systems of thought rest upon assumptions, sometimes called *a prioris* or *foundations*, that, acknowledged or not, can neither be proven nor disproven, yet upon which a system of thought depends. Such is the case with Tolle and Aristotle, in which attending to their foundational commitments can tell us something about how they differ from each other.

Angelic Life, Foundations, and Transcendence

Aristotle calls his most basic assumption the "principle of noncontradiction," which he says is "non hypothetical," which is to say it can neither be proven nor disproven. Aristotle speaks of it as a principle, or a first principle, about "which it is impossible to think falsely"[10] and which is a condition required for any knowledge. The principle he says is "non hypothetical," a hypothesis being something to be proven or disproven. But, as Aristotle admits, his principle of noncontradiction can neither be proven nor disproven; if anything, it is what makes proving or disproving possible but, regarding itself, cannot be proved or disproved. In this way it is not a hypothesis, but neither is it a philosophical a priori, says Nussbaum, if we mean by that a "principle that can be known to hold independently of all experience and all ways of life, all conceptual schemes."[11]

For this reason, Nussbaum points out, when the critics of Aristotle's principle of noncontradiction ask for a proof, Aristotle does not try to prove his principle by using some principle that can be known outside of our human ways of thinking; instead he appeals to what we intuitively know. What is this principle that can neither be proven nor disproven, but upon which Aristotle says all knowledge depends? "Clearly," Aristotle says,

> such a principle is the most certain of all; and what this principle is, we proceed, to state. It is "The same thing cannot at the same time both belong and not belong to the same object and in the same respect." . . . Indeed, this is the most certain of all principles, for it has the specification stated above. For it is impossible for anyone to believe the same thing to be and not to be, as some think Heraclitus says; for one does not necessarily believe what he says.[12]

An example of Aristotle's rule would be to say, "Socrates is a mortal," and then assert, at the same time, "Socrates is a not a mortal." This Aristotle would say is an invalid statement. The principle

---

10. Aristotle, *Metaphysics*, 105b-13.
11. Nussbaum, *Fragility of Goodness*, 254.
12. Aristotle, *Metaphysics*, 1005b20-24.

of noncontradiction brings with it a variety of beliefs about how things work: that indeed there is an order to things, that such an order can be accessed by the human mind on the level of appearances, that the order brings with it a kind of consistency, and that humans ought to work toward consistency.

Aristotle places his principle of noncontradiction in contrast to Heraclitus, a contemporary of Plato, regarding whom "one who does not necessarily believe what he says." And one element of Heraclitus's teaching is what is known as the "law of impermanence of all things," which serves as a foundational principle for Tolle.[13]

This impermanence of all things should not be perceived as "bad" nor should it be avoided for, as Tolle says, "it just is."[14] Such a law has it, that "on the level of form, there is birth and death, creation and destruction, growth and dissolution, or seemingly separate forms. This is reflected everywhere: in the life cycle of a star or planet, a physical body, a tree, a flower; in the rise and fall of nations, political systems, civilizations; and in the inevitable cycles of gain and loss in the life of an individual."[15]

The "inevitable cycles of gain and loss of the individual" are such that one is tempted to assign positive value to the "gain" parts of life—material success, emotional happiness, physical health, independence—while devaluing the "loss" parts of life such as financial insecurity, social isolation, and emotional affliction. To "cling" to the cycles of success, and to resist the cycles of decline is to refuse to go with the "flow of life," and in resisting one brings suffering upon oneself. To go with the "flow of life" means to recognize and embrace the cycles of decline which "make room for new things to arise, or for transformation to happen."[16] Dead, accumulated vegetation needs to be burned so as to make way for the fresh, spiritual growth to happen.

---

13. Tolle, *Power of Now*, 183.
14. Tolle, *Power of Now*, 183.
15. Tolle, *Power of Now*, 183.
16. Tolle, *Power of Now*, 183.

Angelic Life, Foundations, and Transcendence

The cyclical view of time and life is very similar to the Buddha's teaching, regarding which Tolle writes, "All conditions are highly unstable and in constant flux or, as he put it, impermanence is a characteristic of every condition, every situation you will ever encounter in your life. It will change, disappear, or no longer satisfy you."[17] In his teaching on the *dukkha*, the Buddha says that happiness is not separable from suffering, that the two in fact are one. Only time is what makes them appear as separate—that we experience success and happiness at one moment, and later we experience failure and grief. But in fact, says Tolle and the Buddha, they are inseparable in that the seeds of one lay dormant, waiting to germinate, in the other.

This is not to say that one should no longer find enjoyment in the things of this world, says Tolle. We can still appreciate them, but now do so with the knowledge that they cannot deliver on what one ultimately needs—"identity, a sense of permanency, and fulfillment."[18] Once one becomes aware of the impermanent and cyclical nature of things, life takes on an ease where there was once struggle: "Things, people, or conditions now come to you with no struggle or effort on your part, and you are free to enjoy and appreciate them—while they last. All those things, of course, will still pass away, cycles will come and go, but with dependency gone there is no fear of loss anymore. Life flows with ease."[19]

Our question is what becomes of Tolle's unchanging self, a self that participates in pure, eternal Being, but exists at the same time in a reality in which time is cyclical and creation is ever-changing? How does one go with the flow in that changing universe and yet be a constant, unchanged self?

At this point, Aristotle would say that, at the very least, there exists a tension here that requires some further explanation; at most, there exists a contradiction—that you cannot exist in a permanent, unchanging, and timeless state of Being, and at the same time exist in flux, impermanence, changing and becoming.

17. Tolle, *Power of Now*, 184–85.
18. Tolle, *Power of Now*, 186.
19. Tolle, *Power of Now*, 188.

Eckhart Tolle's Hall of Mirrors

Aristotle's principle of noncontradiction is not just a "principle," but it is a way of thinking that values consistency, a consistency that is baked into his entire notion of practical wisdom. To say this is not to deny that there are matters that may appear contradictory but in fact are not. But at the very least, one is obliged to explain how this is the case. Aristotle teaches with one eye on the consistency of his arguments because humans naturally want things to follow, to possess an internal logic that is consistent.

On the other hand, to such an accusation, Tolle has a ready-made response to Aristotle, that he is operating from a place of thought, and that he is dualistic in his thinking—that is, Aristotle is unable to see how we can Be, *and* be in a state of Becoming, at the same time. This disagreement between Aristotle and Tolle is perhaps unresolvable for the reasons stated earlier, that each has their foundational assumptions, or presuppositions that exist beyond logic and provability and disprovability. In response, Aristotle would say that Tolle's non-dualist thinking operates outside of the world of human experience, that within the realm of human experience we make distinctions, are attentive to contradictions, and are inclined toward consistency.

To make his point, Aristotle employs a strategy of getting one's opponent to say something—anything—without feeling obligated to put forth a full-fledged argument. If she does not say anything, then there is no need to take her seriously. By not communicating, she is not one of us. As Aristotle says, "It is comical to look for something to say to someone who won't say anything. A person who is like that, insofar as he is like that, is pretty well like a vegetable."[20] Nussbaum economically completes Aristotle's train of thought as she says, "But if he does say something, something definite, then you can go on to show him that in so doing he is in fact believing and making use of the very principle he attacks. For in order to say something definite he has to be ruling out something else as incompatible; at the very least, the contradictory of what he has asserted."[21]

---

20. Aristotle, *Metaphysics*, 1006a13–15.
21. Nussbaum, *Fragility of Goodness*, 252.

THE METAPHYSICS OF THE ONE AND THE MANY

In terms of metaphysics, the difference between Tolle and Aristotle is how they approach the relationship between the one—non-duality—and the many (the particular, concrete, and disparate objects in human life). Aristotle, so I have argued, starts with the particular and moves his way up to the oneness of non-duality, whereas Tolle (like Plato) begins with the oneness (or non-duality) and works his way down applying it to particulars.

In one sense, both Tolle and Aristotle are engaged in a duality in terms of their philosophical systems—the duality of the particular and the universal. And where they start their thinking (with the particular or the universal) brings with it its own talk and logic. So, in the case of Tolle, who starts with universals, we are treated to a kind of talk that is poetic, abstract, general, and analogical. This is something he must do because the realm of the universal, the non-dual, is, by definition, beyond physicality, beyond substance. We cannot speak of Being (a universal) or Consciousness in the same way we can talk about the objects that exist in human life, in both their material and immaterial forms.

Not only is there a different kind of talk that comes with the priority of universals, but there is a different kind of logic. Universals are, by definition, immaterial. They cannot be picked up, weighed, or measured in the same way a bag of flour from the market can be weighed. In terms of the metaphysical universals, they cannot be talked about directly, but must be spoken about by analogy. For example, we can only say what Being is like, or what Being is not like, but we cannot say de facto what it is. We can say, for example, Being is oneness, or we can say Being is that which unifies all things. We can say, for example, that Being is like pure, white light. It is a light humans cannot see, but we know caries within itself the primary colors that shine on the particulars of human life so that we can see their colors. In this case the talk of a universal, that of Being, as that which sheds light on particulars, allowing humans to interpret in some way the world around us.

Eckhart Tolle's Hall of Mirrors

As I said, where one starts in one's metaphysics—with the universal or the particular—brings with it a kind of talk and logic. Because Tolle begins with (and privileges) the talk of universals, he also thinks in a way in which the many particulars are brought into a kind of harmony. Aristotle, on the other hand, starts with the particular "substances"—objects, events, ideas, activities—that humans experience in their day-to-day lives and draws more general conclusions. This starting place of the particular brings with it its own kind of talk and logic. Aristotle's talk is relatively plain spoken and straightforward, certainly in contrast to Tolle's talk. Because it has to do with particulars and substances, he writes in a way that is descriptive and concrete. When he speaks analogically, it is a way to describe the particulars of a situation.

The universal brings with it its own kind of talk and logic (as we see in Tolle), just as the particular brings with it its own talk and logic (as we see in Aristotle). On the one hand, we can say that this makes sense—that these are distinct and separate orders of reality, in which one cannot use the language and logic of particular objects when speaking of the universal, and vice versa. However, to say this is not to say they are unrelated.

They are related in that they bear upon the other. The universal, for example, represents a whole, so to speak, that contains the particular parts. Or we could say that the many parts make up the whole, in which reality is the word we use to describe the two in relation to each other.

It is fair to say that Tolle and Aristotle share this appreciation of the importance of understanding reality as a universal or whole in relation to the particulars. In this way, they are both nondualists, in the sense that we've been speaking about Tolle.

However Aristotle's commitment for the indispensability of particulars is made clear through many of his texts, in which one can and must arrive at universal ideas or categories through particulars; but this cannot be said the other way around—that one cannot arrive at particulars through universals. And his insistence of the indispensability of the principle of noncontradiction bears witness to this commitment to begin our talk and thinking with what humans can experience and observe in all its particularity.

And yet, as said earlier, it is the whole (the universal) that in turn makes for knowledge, for knowledge is making sense of the parts (the particulars). Making particulars the starting point in the project of understanding reality brings with it a dualism (in the sense that particulars are in contrast to universals). But, for Aristotle, engagement with particulars then leads us to a whole that is singular, but at the same time is a whole that contains both duality and non-duality. The paradox is that particulars are what allow us to form our understanding of the whole, but then that understanding of the whole illuminates the relationship of the parts, including illuminating those parts that stand outside the whole, that which cannot be assimilated into the whole—that which is *other*.

As said earlier, particularity and universality each bring with it a unique talk and logic. Aristotle's principle of noncontradiction reflects his priority of the particular and is a kind of talk and logic that reflects that commitment. Likewise, Tolle's priority of universality brings with it a particular kind of talk and logic. Being, awareness, Consciousness, the hidden harmony, oneness, God, Presence—all of this is a talk that brings with it is a kind of logic and metaphysical claims. And the logic that comes with his priority of universality is one that puts the whole, the universal, in an over-and-against relationship to the particular in which the particular comes out the loser, given that the particulars have been branded from the start by Tolle as deficient, as that which is illusory.

Where Aristotle promotes a trust in and engagement with appearances, Tolle promotes a mistrust—that things are not as they appear; where Aristotle argues that, when we think ethically, we should do so in a way that is in accord with our status as a particular species of animals; in contrast, Tolle argues we are not our physical bodies, that we should think of ourselves with all of creation; where Aristotle argues that particular emotions (such as pity and fear) are necessary to our humanity, Tolle argues that emotions cloud our judgment and should be transcended; where

Aristotle argues that a self is informed by humans relationships, actions, aspirations, and desires, Tolle promotes a notion of a "true self" that is away and by itself in the form of a transcendent "I"; where Aristotle promotes a notion of the human whose existence is precarious, and so requires practical reasoning, membership and cooperation within a political community, Tolle promotes an "I am" that participates in a transcendent consciousness and only then associates itself with others in "enlightened communities"; where Aristotle promotes a notion of a mortality that brings with it storytelling as a means of learning, interpreting, and socialization, Tolle promotes an immortality that equates storytelling with fiction and fantasy, and at odds with an objectivity that comes from pure Consciousness. The list goes on. But in all cases such depreciation of the particular, and privileging the universal has the effect, so I am arguing, of impoverishing our humanness.

There is a moment in which Tolle seems to suggest otherwise—that he is not diminishing the particular—when he writes,

> Although the unmanifested realm of pure consciousness could be considered another dimension, it is not separate from this dimension of form. Form and formlessness interpenetrate. The unmanifested flows into the dimension as awareness, inner space, Presence. How does it do that? Through the human form that becomes conscious and thus fulfills its destiny: The human form was created for this higher purpose, and millions of other forms prepared the ground for it.[22]

This statement suggests that the formlessness of Being informs the emotional, thought, social, and material forms that make up human life, that the formlessness of Being returns to animate the particular forms of earthly life. These are words that monotheists— Christians, Muslims, and Jews—would be in alignment with. But, despite this being said, this statement is in no way determinative of Tolle's overall project. If it were, the emphasis of his writing would not have been on depreciating the particular forms of earthly life, on the one hand, and promoting transcendence, detachment, and

22. Tolle, *New Earth*, 291.

consciousness on the other. If this was determinative of his overall project, his writing would be about the "interpenetration" of form and formlessness. To my mind, such a claim is too little, too late for it is a claim that plays very little role in his overall project.

There are other places where Tolle makes claims that are misleading in terms of his overall project. Regarding the body, he writes,

> On the level of the body, humans are very close to animals. All the basic bodily functions—pleasure, pain, breathing, eating, drinking, defecating, sleeping, the drive to find a mate and procreate, and of course birth and death—we share with the animals. A long time after that their fall from a state of grace and oneness into illusion, humans suddenly woke up in what seemed to be an animal body—and they found this very disturbing—"Don't fool yourself. You are no more than an animal." This seemed to be the truth that was staring them in the face. But it was too disturbing a truth to tolerate. Adam and Eve saw that they were naked, and they became afraid. Unconscious denial of their animal nature set in very quickly. The threat that they might be taken over by powerful instinctual drives and revert back to complete unconsciousness was indeed a very real one. Shame and taboos appeared around certain parts of the body and bodily functions, especially sexuality. The light of their consciousness was not strong enough to make friends with their animal nature, to allow it to be and even to enjoy that aspect of themselves—let alone go deeply into it to find the divine hidden within it, the reality within the illusion. So they did what they had to do. They began to disassociate from their body. They now saw themselves as having a body, rather than just being it.[23]

Tolle's retelling of the garden of Eden story here is to give us an account as to why mortification of the flesh is misguided. But there is much incoherence internal to this passage, as well as its inconsistency with his overall project. Tolle's retelling of the myth has it that, firstly, humans are not animals, but share many animal

23. Tolle, *New Earth*, 113–14.

functions. In such a state, Adam and Eve were unaware or unconscious of their animal functions, living, as it were, in a state of innocence. Such a state of animality, Tolle says, is a state of grace, oneness, and non-illusion (or consciousness). But then Adam and Eve woke up and realized their animal nature and found this disturbing. At this point, Tolle's retelling does not make sense because Adam and Eve are living in animal and bodily forms and are at the same time living a life without illusion, which is to say they are enjoying consciousness. If we have learned anything from Tolle, it is that earthly forms are the source of unconsciousness and illusion for the human person because when we identify with them, they bring with them an instability. But here, Adam and Eve are living in consciousness *and* totally inhabiting earthly forms. This does not make sense as it is inconsistent with the trajectory of Tolle's thought. Then he goes on to write, "Unconscious denial of their animal nature set in very quickly. The threat that they might be taken over by powerful instinctual drives and revert back to complete unconsciousness was indeed a very real one." So here Tolle is saying that their returning to a state of "instinctual drives" is a "real" threat—that such a return is a return to "unconsciousness." This statement is consistent with Tolle's overall arguments—that human behavior directed by instincts, even more than emotions, puts one in a deeply unconsciousness state of affairs, which for Tolle is of course the root of human suffering. But this does not square with Tolle's earlier statement that the "animal functions" Adam and Eve embody are in a state of grace, oneness, and non-illusion. On the one hand, Tolle describes this bodily/instinctual unconsciousness as a "real threat"; on the other hand, he describes the loss of such bodily/instinctual life as a fall from grace and a loss of oneness.

Tolle's goes on to say that "light of their consciousness was not strong enough to make friends with their animal nature, to allow it to be and even to enjoy that aspect of themselves—let alone go deeply into it to find the divine hidden within it, the reality within the illusion." In this way, Tolle introduces the reader to a new imperative, a new project—that of taking human/earthly

Angelic Life, Foundations, and Transcendence

forms—which are, as he has been telling us, illusory—and finding the "reality within the illusion." Such an imperative begs the question: Why not encourage us to find the "reality within the illusion" in terms of the many "external forces"[24] he has been sounding the alarm against? Why not find the "reality within the illusion" in "the false mind-made self,"[25] "the dreadful affliction of thinking,"[26] "the totally separate 'other,'"[27] the "illusion" of pain,[28] the "delusion of time,"[29] and "the illusion that you are a body"?[30]

One can go on with the list of illusions in which there is a hidden divine reality for Adam and Eve to "find the divine hidden within." But, like the previous quote regarding the interpenetration of form and formlessness, retelling the garden of Eden myth may give the appearance that Tolle suggests some kind of embrace of the particular, in the form of the physical body, for as he says of Adam and Eve's self-consciousness of their bodies, "they now saw themselves having a body, rather than just being it."[31] But after educating us in the misguided efforts of medieval monastics (and the Buddha himself) in their practices of bodily mortification, he reminds Adam and Eve (and, therefore, us) that, on the one hand, "you are your body," one that is an "animal body," and that Adam and Eve should "enjoy that aspect of themselves"; on the other hand, Tolle writes, "the body that you can see and touch is only a thin illusory veil. Underneath it lies the invisible inner body, the doorway to Being, into Life Unmanifested. Through the inner body, you are inseparably connected to this unmanifested one life—birthless, deathless, eternally present. Through the inner body, you are forever one with God."[32]

24. Tolle, *Power of Now*, 10.
25. Tolle, *Power of Now*, 15.
26. Tolle, *Power of Now*, 14.
27. Tolle, *Power of Now*, 15.
28. Tolle, *Power of Now*, 36.
29. Tolle, *Power of Now*, 48.
30. Tolle, *Power of Now*, 198.
31. Tolle, *Power of Now*, 114.
32. Tolle, *Power of Now*, 116.

Given Tolle's philosophy of the body, one wonders why he would have trouble with the bodily mortification he criticizes. After all, would not such mortification of the physical body encourage one's spiritual focus to move from the dense, physical body to the pure, luminous inner body that is "forever one with God" in much the same way that, as he argues elsewhere, suffering will speed up one's rejection of earthly forms and movement to Being and transcendence?

TOLLE AND ARISTOTLE ON NATURE

The many criticisms of Tolle in this book share a common element—that Tolle privileges the abstract and universal at the expense of the particular. I would like to make one final example of this dynamic by employing Tolle's use of the word "nature." "Like the Taoist sages of ancient China," he writes, "Jesus likes to draw our attention to nature because he sees a power at work in it that humans have lost touch with. . . . That is to say, that while nature is a beautiful expression of the evolutionary impulse of the universe, when humans become aligned with the intelligence that underlies it, they will express that same impulse on a higher more wonderful level."[33] Consistent with Tolle's overall project, his engagement with the natural world is on a universal level (if not cosmic), that of the "evolutionary impulse of the universe" with which we are to align ourselves if we are to be become agents for improvement "on a higher more wonderful level." Elsewhere Tolle writes that non-egoic action joins and does not separate. Actions "are not for 'my' country, but for all of humanity. Not for 'my' religion but the emergence of consciousness in all human beings, not for 'my' species but for all sentient beings and all of nature."[34]

In contrast, Aristotle spent much time studying animal species in their natural environments. He was particularly interested in marine mammals such as dolphins (and classified them as

---

33. Tolle, *New Earth*, 268–69.
34. Tolle, *New Earth*, 290.

such—mammals, and not fish), but also crustaceans, land mammals, and insects. Aristotle's attention to particular animal species and their interaction with other species and the environments they inhabit, allowed him to make valuable contributions to what we moderns call "environmental science." Aristotle might not be considered an environmentalist in the activist sense, for the degradation to the environment we experience today is of course on a much greater scale than in his time. But his attention to particular species in their native habitats provides us with a salient example of his movement from the particular to the universal, a movement that prevented him from employing a notion of "nature" off by itself and without context. Such a notion of "nature" is a bit like the word "consciousness" in that it suggests an all-inclusive description of "what is." But such a totality is, as Aristotle says, off and outside of human experience and thus, like Plato's forms, unhelpful.

David Abram, speaking of the philosopher Maurice Merleau-Ponty (a fellow graduate student in phenomenology with Edith Stein, whose notion of the body we discussed in the first chapter), argues for a notion of experience that begins with the temporal human body (and not Tolle's inner body) that "demolishes any hope that philosophy might eventually provide a complete picture of reality (for any such total account of 'what is' requires a mind or consciousness that stands outside of existence, whether to compile the account or, finally, to receive and comprehend it). Yet by this same move he [Merleau-Ponty] opens, at last, the possibility of a truly authentic phenomenology, a philosophy which would strive, not to explain the world as if from outside, but to give voice to the world from our experienced situation within it, recalling us to our participation in the here-and-now, rejuvenating our sense of wonder at the fathomless things, events and powers that surround us on every hand."[35]

Tolle's talk of action that is "not for 'my' species but for all sentient beings and all of nature" is at a level of abstraction that affords us little in terms of how to be responsible human animals because by depreciating our human animality he places us outside

35. Abram, *Spell of the Sensuous*, 47.

"nature"—outside, as it were, looking in. But such looking in upon nature from outside, once again, from the point of view of angels who, as Wenders had it in his movie *Wings of Desire*, are unable to see and experience particulars. On the other hand, we animals, human and nonhuman alike, exist in particular biomes or habitats such as deserts, mountains, along woodlands, salt marshes, and on the plains and prairies. As Abram puts it,

> The earth of our direct experience is not that of a blue marble, flecked with white, mapped and monitored by innumerable satellites. Rather, it is the particular place where I find myself, the tangible terrain that I engage with my muscles, whose horizons beckon my eyes and whose tangled rhythms nourish my listening ears. It is this high windswept valley dreaming of rains that seldom come; or that rolling woodland overrun with suburban subdivisions and marauding deer; or that coastal estuary cradling your metropolis where peregrines nest atop the tall bridges and mussel beds seeded by schoolchildren sieve industrial pollutants from the tides. Only by being deeply here, in and of this place, am I palpably connected to every other place. However much I may be concerned by events unfurling on the far side of the globe, and however insistently those happenings shove themselves through my various screens and headsets, my primary responsibility must be to the realm that I ceaselessly inhabit with the whole of my creaturely flesh, and to the palpable relationships that I sustain in this realm.[36]

Just as we inhabit but a particular body, we inhabit a particular place; in this way our task is to come to learn about and love this particular body in its inhabiting this particular place. That is not to say we cannot know and love other places in the way we know and love our own. Such knowing and loving amounts to a kind of spirituality, but it is not a spirituality of transcending to a place of pure consciousness, off by itself; better said, it is a spirituality of descending. Such descending is a way of being in the world, in a particular part of the world, that brings with it many

---

36. Abram, *Spell of the Sensuous*, 284.

responsibilities; attending to the particular beauty and challenges to that place may not immunize us from the precarious nature of animal life, but it will bring us into alignment with our particular bodies that navigate particular places at a particular time.

Bibliography

Abram, David. *The Spell of the Sensuous: Perception and Language in a More Than Human World*. New York: Vintage, 1997.
Aristotle. *Aristotle: Selected Works*. Grinnell, IA: Peripatetic, 1982.
———. *Nicomachean Ethics*. Indianapolis: Bobbs-Merrill Educational, 1962.
Heidegger, Martin. *Being and Time*. New York: Harper and Row, 1962.
Lasch, Christopher. *The Culture of Narcissism: American Life in an Age of Diminishing Expectations*. New York: Norton, 1979.
MacIntyre, Alasdair. *Dependent Rational Animals: Why Human Beings Need the Virtues*. Chicago: Open Court, 1999.
Mead, George Herbert. *Mind, Self, and Society: The Definitive Edition*. Chicago: University of Chicago Press, 2015.
Nussbaum, Martha. *Anger and Forgiveness: Resentment, Generosity, Justice*. Oxford: Oxford University Press, 2016.
———. *The Fragility of Goodness: Luck and Ethics in Greek Tragedy and Philosophy*. Cambridge: Cambridge University Press, 1986.
———. *Love's Knowledge: Essays on Philosophy and Literature*. Oxford: Oxford University Press, 1990.
Plato. *The Republic: A Dialogue on Justice*. Kshetra, 2016
———. *The Symposium*. London: Penguin Books, 1999.
Ricoeur, Paul. *Oneself as Another*. Chicago: University of Chicago Press, 1992.
Stein, Edith. *On the Problem of Empathy*. Translated by Waltraut Stein. Washington, DC: Institute of Carmelite Studies, 1989.
Tolle, Eckhart. *A New Earth: Awakening to Your Life's Purpose*. New York: Penguin, 2016.
———. *The Power of Now: A Guide to Spiritual Enlightenment*. Vancouver, BC: Namaste, 2004.
———. "The Prison of Narcissism." YouTube video, 13:09. Posted March 30, 2021. https://www.youtube.com/watch?v=dLLB7daSttY&t=490s&ab_channel=AfterSkool.
———. "What Can We Learn through Betrayal?" YouTube video, 10:44. Posted August 26, 2014. https://www.youtube.com/watch?v=tXIJQpYF51c&ab_channel=EckhartTolle.

BIBLIOGRAPHY

Wenders, Wim. *The Logic of Images: Essays and Conversations.* London: Faber and Faber, 1991.

www.ingramcontent.com/pod-product-compliance
Lightning Source LLC
Chambersburg PA
CBHW050831160426
43192CB00010B/1988